KIPPER
&
FRIENDS

Copyright Bill Ames 2020

Second edition January 2021

Table of Contents

Dedication	5
Acknowledgements	7
Prologue	9
Chapter 1- Pre-history	13
Chapter 2- Boundaries Road	23
Chapter 3- Chart Way	45
Chapter 4- Benting Mead	61
Chapter 5- New kid on the block	81
Chapter 6- Difficult Times	109
Chapter 7- Rescued	141
Chapter 8- Eastbourne (Harbour)	163
Chapter 9- Eastbourne (Seafront)	171
Epilogue	177

To Sally,

For our continued friendship over so many of our ups and downs over the years.

Love, Eleanor

June 2021

DEDICATION

This book is dedicated to

ILEANA MACMILLAN

She has been our friend for over forty five years. We are grateful for her friendship and for her support in looking after our home and animals. She did this over a period of more than fifteen years.

ACKNOWLEDGEMENTS

I am indebted to my wife Ruth for coming up with the idea of recording our experiences with our several cats and dogs through their eyes. She was particularly attached to the Siamese cats each of whom had their peculiar characteristics and never failed to be astonished by their antics.

My thanks also to my son Edward for his helpful comments and for encouraging me to refer other sources for help in constructing this narrative.

While this book is based on true events, the names of the human characters have been changed to protect their identities.

PROLOGUE

Although my wife and I had had pets in our respective family homes at various times while we were growing up, we did not have a pet in our own home until we bought our first house in England. Even then when we got a dog it was as a pet for our son. This did not work out so we switched to cats, one of whom, Hercules, is the narrator of the first few chapters. Our son brought a Siamese kitten Ella into the family and three of her offspring figure prominently in this book.

When we moved to a large property we got a Rough Collie male dog named Bertie. A second dog, Kipper, a German Shepherd male, joined him a few months later. Kipper is the second narrator of this book. As the property was reasonably secluded we got the dogs partly for security.

My wife had become very fond of the Siamese cats as each of them was a very interesting character as portrayed in this book. When the last of them passed away, she rescued Nancy, the final narrator who was the longest lived and spent the last fifteen years of her life as our companion. During Nancy's time with us we rescued Oliver, a Siamese Blue Point male aged ten who lived with us for six years.

This book is a history of our family over a period of over forty years and is factual although the names of some people have been changed. I hope that readers will find the story as seen through the eyes of animals interesting. From what I observed of their behaviour, I have tried to imagine what they may have thought about themselves and the humans in their lives. My intention is to bring to life the characters of each pet animal through the many anecdotes contained in the book.

HERCULES

Chapter 1 - Pre-history

Hello! I am Hercules. No, not the strong man of Greek mythology, but a black and white tom cat - you can call me "Herky". I like to think that I am the feline equivalent of my namesake, big and strong but gentle.

I was born in 1973 but over the years I learned about the history of my human family and I think it is appropriate that I should start by narrating some of the information I had gathered retrospectively. In the rest of this narrative I will refer to my human parents as Mum and Dad or as "my parents".

My parents had first come to England from Sri Lanka (then known as Ceylon) in August 1962 when Dad was transferred to the London Office of the bank he worked for. As air travel was too expensive they had come to England by ship, the voyage taking twenty two days. After a few months living in a bedsit in Bayswater,

West London, they had moved to a flat in Balham, South London in December that year. Within six months of their arrival, they had been joined in London by Mum's parents (Grandpa and Grandma) and her siblings Winston, Marie and Jim.

The first winter that my parents spent in England had been one of the severest and longest on record. They had been returning after lunch with friends in neighbouring Tooting Bec on Boxing day 1962, when for the first time they saw snow falling. It had snowed heavily for several days after that and the snow had later turned to ice which did not thaw completely for three months. Mum who was pregnant with Ron had slipped on the ice and fallen a few times but had fortunately not hurt herself or the baby. Smog had also been a big problem in London at the time and I once heard Mum telling someone that she had walked into a red pillar box in the smog because she could not see it.

Ron was born in July 1963. He had been placed with a child minder at three months old when Mum went back to work. I heard Mum bemoaning the fact several times over the years that she bitterly regretted having to leave such a young child to be looked after by someone else. She had to go back to work for financial reasons and it really broke her heart to be parted from her baby so early.

Dad had completed his Diploma in Banking in 1964 and had completed Part I of a B Sc (Economics) degree from the University of London the same year for which he had been studying part time through a correspondence course. As a part time student he could not sit for Part II for a further three years. Dad was supposed to return to Ceylon in 1966 but had been granted an extension of one year to enable him to complete his degree. Hector, a son of Grandpa's brother Harry had come to settle in England 1964.

My parents had tried to see as much of the country as possible during their four year stay. They had been taking short camping holidays or staying in bed and breakfast accommodation during Bank Holiday weekends. They used to be accompanied by Mum's parents (Grandpa and Grandma), Winston and his wife Lesley, Marie and often by Jim and Hector.

Dad's youngest brother Guy had come over in March 1965 with his wife Charmaine to settle in England. Dad's father had visited later that year on holiday and had been given leave to stay on indefinitely. Mum had started working in advertising and was studying for her professional examinations too. Guy had suggested that Mum and Dad should stay on in England as the cost of living and the availability of essentials had worsened since they had left Ceylon.

That summer Dad had organised a fortnight's motoring and camping holiday in Europe in a hired ten seater van. The touring party had consisted of Mum, Dad, Ron, Grandma, Guy, Charmaine, Marie, Jim and Hector. Crossing by ferry from Dover to Ostend, they had spent time in Belgium, The Netherlands, West Germany, Switzerland and France. Grandpa had gone to Russia by train via several Eastern European countries, accompanying a group of schoolboys as a photographer during the same period.

My parents had gone on another motoring and camping holiday, to France the following summer (1966). They had been accompanied by Ron, Winston, Lesley and Hector. As Dad had passed his driving test, he had been able to share the driving with Winston. They had camped initially in Versailles but after enduring two days of persistent rain, they had decided to go south. After an overnight stop, they had camped about twenty miles from Nice for the rest of their holiday (about ten days). They had driven down daily to the beach in Nice or

Cannes where three year old Ron had loved to frolic in the sea. Unfortunately, Ron had been caught unawares by a wave which knocked him over. This traumatic incident had made him so afraid of water that he would not even enter a swimming pool until he went to boarding school four years later .

It was not until 1967 that my parents had finally decided to settle in England so Dad had to resign from the bank. He found employment with a company in Mitcham, Surrey. That year Dad had obtained a degree in Economics from the University of London and Mum had passed her professional examination in Advertising the following year. My parents had bought a three bed-roomed terraced house in Balham, not far from where they used to rent, and moved there in September 1967. This is the house in which I was born.

Dad's father who had been living with Guy and Charmaine, had moved in with my parents and Ron about a month later. He had not been in very good health and had passed away in December 1967. Ron had started school at St. Mary's Church of England Primary School in Balham in September 1968.

The following year, Mum, Dad and Ron accompanied by Charmaine (who had separated from Guy) had flown to Ceylon on a charter flight to spend Christmas and New Year there. In Ceylon, Charmaine stayed with her father while Dad's brother Jay put the others up in his home. They spent a whole month in Ceylon. Grandpa, Grandma, Winston and Lesley who had driven overland from England in two cars, were there at the same time.

My parents had spent most of their month's holiday visiting and introducing Ron, now aged six, to their relatives. They had been able to spend a week touring the hill country due to the generosity of a good friend who had provided them with a chauffeur driven car and accommodation. While at Jay's house, Ron had thoroughly enjoyed playing with Jay's son George who was just under four, and some neighbours' children.

A year later, Mum, Dad and Ron had gone to Majorca for ten days during the Easter break. This had been their first "package holiday". They had been fortunate to meet a family from Leicester staying in the same hotel whose son and daughter were around Ron's age so he enjoyed their company.

Mum's parents had returned to England in 1971 and moved in with the family. Grandpa and Grandma were in the house when I was born. Marie came to England in 1975 and a few months after her arrival the three of them rented a flat and moved out.

Over the years I learnt about my human family's previous pets. Their first pet, a bitch named Susie, had had a litter of five pups who were found new homes. Susie had then been sterilised. As both Mum and Dad were at work all day and could not find the time for walking Susie, they had decided to find her a new home. Susie had been adopted by some circus folk who were looking for a pet dog.

As cats are less dependent on humans than dogs, my mother Tammy had entered the household as a replacement for Susie and as a pet for Ron. The house which was a mid-terrace, had had its share of rats and mice which disappeared due to Tammy's efforts. Before giving birth to me, Tammy had had a litter of two kittens both of whom were found new homes. I was the only kitten in the next litter. For some unknown reason, Tammy would not give me milk so Mum had to feed me cow's milk.

Chapter 2 - Boundaries Road

I was born on 14th November 1973 which I consider to be an historic day, the day on which Her Majesty Queen Elizabeth II's only daughter HRH Princess Anne married Captain Mark Phillips. It was also the twenty fifth birthday of the Princess' older brother HRH Prince Charles, Prince of Wales. My mother was a black and white cat called Tammy who was quite wild and preferred to spend her time outdoors and even sleep outside, coming in only to be fed.

When I was born, the family lived in a three bedroomed terraced house in South London with a small rear garden and a basement. The household consisted of Mum and Dad, their son Ron a young boy of ten, and Mum's parents (Grandpa and Grandma).

Ron used to regularly disappear for about five days and return for a couple of days which quite puzzled me. I later learned that he was a weekly boarder in a Preparatory School near Reigate. My parents had not been happy with Ron's progress at St. Mary's, the local Church of England School where he had spent two years. They had decided to make him a weekly boarder at the age of seven. It so happened that he was at home the day I was born because he was enjoying a holiday declared in honour of the Princess' marriage.

Unusually I had no brothers or sisters in the same litter and inexplicably my mother Tammy rejected me. Although Tammy had bonded with and fed the two kittens from her previous litter, she refused to let me suckle so Mum had to feed me cow's milk using a pipette. I later started drinking from a saucer. I enjoyed being the family's new "baby".

I was lucky that my Mum and Dad decided to keep me as Tammy's earlier kittens had been re-homed. I think Mum had felt sorry for me because Tammy had rejected me and I could not have survived if I had not been hand-fed. After I was born Tammy was sterilised.

Because Tammy had rejected me, Mum spoilt me rotten. She used to cuddle me a lot and I used to spend hours on her lap while she watched television. She later taught me how to beg. If she showed me something that I liked to eat, I would stand on my hind legs and put my paws out to indicate that I wanted it. My favourite treat was a raw egg. I was fed mainly on tinned cat food. I was neutered when I was about a year old.

Mum and Dad used to comment that our terraced house had been infested with mice before Tammy arrived. She had turned out to be a good mouser. She was so wild that she used to resist being picked up and used to struggled loose. Tammy spent most of her time outdoors while I was content to stay mainly in the house and venture out only occasionally. The garden was quite small so I used to have to sneak out to adjoining properties for my adventures. When I grew up I had hardly any mousing to do and was only occasionally called upon to perform this duty.

Tammy befriended many local cats and used to bring them in to the house. I liked having the house to myself so I acted as if I owned it. When I grew older I made sure Tammy's friends did not enter the house. How dare they? As I spent most of my time at ground level and to save me looking up all the time, I sometimes relied on my other senses to recognise people. I could tell each different member of the household from their footsteps or voices and, in close proximity, by their smell. I could even identify them from a few yards away by looking at their footwear. I used to rub myself against a person's leg if I wanted to be picked up. Mum, Dad and Ron soon got used to this method of communication and used to respond without hesitation.

When I was fully grown I was a big cat weighing over sixteen pounds. The mantel shelf in the front room had several ornaments and I tried to impress Mum and Dad by weaving in and out of these ornaments without knocking them over. I could see the alarm on their faces when they first saw me jump up on the mantel shelf but they soon got used to my showing off.

I loved sunning myself in the back garden and wandering into our neighbours' gardens to explore. I did not particularly fancy going on to the road in front of our house as there was a lot of traffic. Our garden was back to back with that of a house in the parallel road whose occupants used to throw a lot of litter into their garden. My parents used to sometimes find some unmentionable items thrown over the fence by them in our garden too.

Although Ron saw me only weekends, he was very fond of me. Tammy had been introduced to the household as a pet for Ron but she was wild, hated being picked up and was seldom in the house so Ron turned his attention to me. He was very gentle when he used to pick me up and cuddle me and talk to me. I became more affectionate towards Ron as I grew up and sometimes used to go up to him and ask to be picked up or wander into his room and lie on his bed..

As I said before, the school where Ron was a weekly boarder was the last of the three they had been to in their quest. They had visited it on a Saturday afternoon in July when the boys were enjoying themselves in the swimming pool. Ron was interviewed by the Headmaster who tested his reading and numeric abilities. The Headmaster had commented that Ron had a vivid imagination. He wanted Ron to come back in six weeks after mastering his "twelve times" table. When leaving after his interview, Ron had expressed a preference for this school so he had been fortunate to be admitted in September after a second interview.

Ron had been afraid of water since his unnerving experience of being knocked over by a wave in the sea in Nice when he was three. As swimming was compulsory at his school, he had reluctantly entered the pool. During his second summer, the Matron had found Ron avoiding swimming lessons. The teacher in charge had been asked why he did not spot that Ron was missing from the pool. The teacher had replied that there had been three dark skinned boys the previous summer and that there were three this summer too, so he had assumed that they were the same boys. He had not realised that the the two Fernando boys from the previous year had been joined by their younger brother making up the three, so Ron was able to abscond. Ron had overcome his fear of water and actually enjoyed learning to swim.

When Ron first joined his prep school they had lessons on Saturday mornings so Mum or Dad used to pick him up around noon to bring him home for the weekend. After about two years the school had decided not to have Saturday classes, so it was much easier for Dad to drive down after work to pick Ron up on Friday evenings. In the summer Dad used to play cricket on Sundays for his company so Mum had to drive Ron down to his school on Sunday evenings.

During his last two years at his prep school, Dad used to pick up Ron and another boy on Fridays and deliver the latter to his home in Croydon. That boy's parents would collect Ron on Sunday evenings for the return trip to school to save Mum and Dad the journey.

On several occasions during my life of over sixteen years, I observed incidents in the household which I found amusing or just interesting and sometimes even alarming. I will be recounting some anecdotes of those incidents which enriched my life with the family. Along the way I also pieced together the recent history of my human family.

Mum's brother Jim had moved back to Balham, had married Susan and they had three daughters who visited often. I allowed them to pet me, but I used to simply walk away if they began to get a little rough. About once a month the family (including Grandpa, Grandma, Tammy and me), used to go to Henlow in Bedfordshire to spend the weekend with Mum's cousin Cheryl and her family. I really hated the car journey. Cheryl had two little children, a girl and a boy who also wanted to pet me. It was lucky that I was fond of little children myself so this was not a problem.

One Friday evening the entire family was in the dining room waiting for dinner which was being cooked by Grandma, to be served. The black and white television was switched on and I was having a quiet snooze in a corner of the dining room when I suddenly heard an argument.

Raised voices woke me from my reverie and I sensed something bad was going to happen and cowered in my corner. I gathered that Ron had breezed into the room while Grandpa was watching his favourite show "Hawai-Five-O" and changed the channel on the television. Everyone in the room had been surprised and Grandpa had been very upset. I had just woken up when I heard the following conversation.

"What are you doing son? Grandpa was watching his show."
"Dad, I am away from home all week and do not have a chance of watching any television programmes, so I must be given priority at the weekend".
Dad was quite taken aback at this argument but saw the logic of it.
"I tend to agree with you son, but could you please let Grandpa watch his show today?".

Ron was adamant and so Grandpa went off in a huff. Grandpa had been a teacher and was not used to children having their own way. Grandpa was very angry that Dad had given in to the wishes of a young boy rather than support him. As the household had only one television set, Grandpa had to forego his programme that evening.

Whenever there was a Bank Holiday Monday during term time, Ron used to invite one of his school friends to spend the long weekend with us. One Friday when Dad went to collect Ron and a friend for the long weekend, he was surprised that the Principal refused to let Ron's friend go. The Principal had explained to Dad that Ron's friend had a brother in the school who had not been invited out by anyone to spend the long weekend at their home. The Principal he felt that it was not fair that one brother had to stay behind in the school while the other enjoyed the hospitality of a friend's family.

Dad had no hesitation in inviting both brothers and so the Smith brothers came for the weekend. That Sunday morning after breakfast, Mum made the following announcement.

"I am cooking a curry for lunch, what do you boys like to eat?".

"Yes please" replied the Smith brothers in unison. This took everyone by surprise, Ron more than the others because he did not eat curry.

"Why do you want to eat that rubbish?" Ron asked his friends before he settled for sausages and mashed potato. It transpired that the boys' parents lived in Kenya where Mr Smith worked as an engineer and that their Indian cook regularly had curry on the menu.

Ron appears to have enjoyed his stint at his prep school where he won his colours at rugby football and soccer and excelled at cricket. Ron also acted in two school plays, playing the parts of Lucius in "Julius Caesar" and Bassanio in "The Merchant of Venice". In his fourth year he won the prize for the best Christmas story "Werewolf's Christmas", beating boys who were two years above him. Ron was made a Prefect in his final year and was expected to wear long trousers. The school cap was replaced by a "Boater" for Prefects.

As Tammy used to come into the house only at meal time, I was effectively the only pet in the household. This suited me fine. I was rarely called upon to perform my duty as a mouser as Tammy had virtually eradicated rats and mice when she first arrived. I was very content with my life although there was not much of a garden to wander about in. This meant I had to trespass into neighbouring properties and sometimes had things thrown at me by the neighbours. I soon learnt which gardens were safe and which neighbours were hostile and adapted my behaviour accordingly.

Dad's brother Guy had divorced Charmaine and re-married, and was living close by in Tooting with his family. He had a stepson called Dan who was about four years younger than Ron. Guy used to bring Dan to play with Ron at the weekends and on some Saturday mornings Dad used to take the two boys to a local cinema. Dan never befriended me. My parents used to have parties every three months or so in our house for their extended family. The attendees used to be their siblings with their spouses, and Mum's cousins and their partners.

Mum and Dad had made friends with the Rajan's who lived in nearby Tooting Broadway. Karen and Ken Ranjan also hailed from Sri Lanka and had two boys Rohan and Sharm. Rohan was just a year younger than Ron while Sharm was about three years younger. During the school holidays Dad used to drop Ron off at the Rajan's house in Tooting on his way to work in Mitcham and Ron used to spend all day there. Karen used to drive the boys about, taking them to various activities and even the cinema and Dad used to collect Ron on his way home from work. In Ron's early years of boarding he used to spend the school holidays with Mum's cousin Charmaine and her husband in Kent.

Mum had been unwell due to the pressures of her responsible job in advertising and wanted to take a break from it. At the time I was born Mum was running a fashion shop in Norbury. The shop was a failure, so she sublet the premises after ten months and joined another advertising agency in London.

I have said before that I was a proud cat and I thought I was privileged to belong to such a kind and loving family. Like all cats I used to love cleaning myself. I had a very glossy black and white coat and took particular pride in keeping it that way all the time. Visitors and passersby used to remark on the condition of my coat and this made both my parents and me very proud and happy.

In summer 1975 Mum started running her own advertising business from home. I was happy that Mum was home all day because I used to be quite lonely when Mum and Dad both went to work and Tammy was always on the loose. Dad had been unhappy in his job for some time. He started a new less responsible job in Feltham, Middlesex in December 1975. This meant he had a longer journey to work and had to travel by train. As Mum was working from home, Ron was delighted that he could stay at home during the school holidays rather than be farmed out to friends and relatives.

While working full time, Jim had qualified as an Automotive Engineer and Road Transport Engineer and was holding a responsible job in the Ministry of Transport as a Vehicle Inspector. Susan worked in the Civil Service. Jim and Susan decided it was better for their three daughters aged eight, seven and three to grow up in another country and they emigrated to New Zealand. I gathered that this country was very far away almost on the other side of the world.

Ron passed his Common Entrance examination and was admitted to a school in Sussex in September 1976 as a full boarder. He was allowed to come home for one weekend each month and even then only on a Saturday afternoon. Ron was lucky to have one of his classmates from his preparatory school assigned to the same school House as he. In November Dad moved jobs again after less than a year and started a new and more senior job in Sutton, Surrey. His new position was that of a Computer Projects Manager (equivalent to a Senior Executive Officer in the Civil Service).

Mum's parents retired from their jobs in 1977 and although quite elderly (Grandpa was nearly seventy years old), they drove overland in a Morris Marina car to Sri Lanka where they had decided to build a house and spend their retirement. I learned to my astonishment that this intrepid couple had already made this journey overland in an Austin 1100 car in 1969. They had been accompanied on that occasion by their older son Winston and his wife who had travelled in their own car.

The Grand National horse race was being run one Saturday when Ron had come home for the weekend. My parents used to have the occasional flutter had decided wanted to place bets on this race. Ron also looked at the race card and spotted a horse called "Lucius". Ron had played the part of Lucius, one of Caesar's servants, in a production of "Julius Caesar" when he was at his prep school. Ron asked whether he could place a bet on this horse which was an outsider, and despite advice from Mum and Dad to place an each way bet, Ron insisted that he bet one pound of his pocket money on a straight win. Lucius came home as the winner at odds of fourteen to one. I heard Dad remarking one day that this horse never won another race.

Helped by an assistant, Mum worked from home for three years before she rented an office in Oxford Street, London in 1978 and moved her businesses there so I was on my own again most of the day. Mum, Dad and Ron accompanied by Mum's cousin John, decided to spend Christmas 1978 in Los Angeles, California with one of Grandma's relatives and were away for two weeks. Tammy and I were left in a cattery for the first time. Although we shared the same cage, neither of us, particularly Tammy who was essentially an outdoor cat, liked being in a small enclosure. I dreaded to think that this could become a regular occurrence.

One weekend in early 1979 I was having an afternoon nap in Mum and Dad's bedroom when I was awakened by hearing Ron's voice. He had come in to speak to his parents.

"Mum, Dad, I have been boarding since I was seven years old (he was now nearly sixteen) and I think it is time I lived at home and got to know my parents. I would like to leave my present school at the end of the summer term after sitting my GCE "O" level examinations." This request came as quite a surprise to his parents but they too had missed having Ron at home so they addressed the problem seriously.

Mum and Dad had to choose a school for Ron's sixth form studies but they were not too keen on any of the local sixth forms colleges. Mum remembered that some of Ron's prep school classmates had transferred to Reigate Grammar School when it became independent in 1975 and thought it would be a good idea for him to be re-united with them. Ron gained a place at Reigate Grammar School so Mum and Dad began looking for a house in that area.

My parents took a day off work and drove down to Reigate to look for a house. By the end of the day they had decided on a house and made an offer that was accepted. Dad encountered some difficulty arranging a mortgage as the new house was much more expensive than our present one.

A few weeks later their solicitor informed my parents that the vendor had withdrawn from the sale of the house in Reigate and had placed it on the market at a higher price and that no further offer would be accepted from them. This left them in a quandary as Ron had already been given a place at Reigate Grammar School. When they received an offer for our present house, Dad instructed their solicitor to send a signed contract for the new asking price together with a cheque for the ten percent deposit to the Reigate vendor's solicitors. Faced with "a bird in the hand" the vendor agreed to sell to Mum and Dad.

Chapter 3 - Chart Way

We moved in June 1979 to a four bedroomed detached house in Reigate which was close enough to Ron's school that he was able to walk home to have his lunch. Tammy and I were fairly comfortable on the car journey to Reigate which took about one hour. When we turned up in Reigate accompanied by our removals van, the vendor's estate agent refused to give Dad the keys to our new home because our solicitor had not turned up from London with the bank draft for the balance of the purchase price.

We had to hang around for over two hours and although I was normally quite laid back, I was getting very tired and agitated being confined in a pet carrier. Tammy was restless because she was basically a wild cat and I think it would have been worse for her. After our arrival, we were confined to the house for over a week, so we had to use the litter tray to relieve ourselves. It is said that cats can find their way back home from far away so perhaps my parents thought it safer that we cats realised that this was our new home before we were let out in the garden.

I considered myself a special cat. After all how many cats can boast of being the only kitten born in a litter? I was also special in that my parents decided not to give me away as they had my half siblings from Tammy's previous litter. I was so privileged to be hand reared and loved so much by my Mum whom I adored.

The move to Reigate meant that both my parents had to travel further to work. Dad's drive to Sutton was straightforward, but Mum had to take the train from Sutton to London and then take a bus to her office. Dad used to drop her off at Sutton railway station in the morning and collect her in the evening and drive back to Reigate. Mum used to cook dinner on her return at around seven thirty although Ron helped by having a meal ready on some days. After dinner they would do some decorating in the new house.

I was very excited to find that the garden was much bigger than the one in Balham and was delighted with the move. Our previous garden had no trees in it so I was very happy to see three largish trees in our new garden and loved running up them to lie in wait for birds. Unfortunately, Mum and Dad had these trees cut down later, much to my disappointment.

Soon after we moved to Reigate a middle aged couple, both teachers from London, moved in next door. The man used to talk to me when he saw me wandering about, particularly if he thought I was straying too far from home. Perhaps he was not aware that cats are noted for their cleverness in finding their way home even from several miles away. I heard him tell my Mum one day "Whenever I meet this Herbert in the street I tell him to go home". Mum was quite amused by his language.

The elderly gentleman who was our immediate neighbour on the other side, was not very friendly and used to shoo me from his garden if he saw me there. I don't think he liked cats or any animals for that matter. I used to watch this neighbour in his garden and wait for him to go indoors before sneaking into his garden to do my business.

Our house had a small front garden as well so when it was sunny I used to sometimes sit there and watch the world go by. I noticed that the road in front was very much quieter than the one in Balham, so I used to sometimes walk along the pavement. I must admit I was a bit haughty and walked with my head held high and a measured tread. My body language suggested that I was someone special and people used to stop to look at me as I wandered along with my nose in the air and a supercilious expression on my face. Sometimes passersby used to stop and talk to me and even stroke me.

The family went off on a holiday to Sri Lanka in December 1979 and put Tammy and me in a cattery. When they returned and were watching television, I stood in the middle of the room and told them off in no uncertain terms for placing us in a cattery again so soon after the first time. After all, enough was enough. To make sure that my parents were still in the house and had not gone away again, I used to jump on their bed at night and walk over their faces.

In 1980 the family decided to carry out some major alterations to the house and a builder called Tony used to come with an assistant to do the alterations while Mum and Dad were away at work. This disturbed my peace for several weeks and I was forced to seek sanctuary in adjoining gardens. Luckily it was summer time so it was quite pleasant to be outdoors. I loved lying on my back in the garden on sunny days to warm my belly. Ron was now a day boy and used to come home for his lunch, often accompanied by a classmate. He was very fond of me and used to pick me up and cuddle me if I was around when he came home.

Tony's dog used to come with him and spend most of the day lying in the back of Tony's pick up truck. Tony liked animals and used to talk to me sometimes during his many tea breaks. Some time that year Tammy went missing and was never seen again. She used to run across the road in front of our house all the time so it is possible she may have been run over and killed.

Life returned to normal after the building alterations had been done. As Tammy had disappeared, I was now the sole pet in the household and I thoroughly enjoyed my status. Mum continued to keep me on her lap and cuddle me quite often although I had been fully grown for several years. I used to sleep with my parents on their bed whenever I wanted to.

Mum had to leave her office in London in 1981 as the owners wished to re-develop the site. I was delighted when she decided to work from home again. This move coincided with Ron leaving school after sitting his GCE 'A' Level examinations, so he started working for Mum whose business was now based in our front bedroom.

Jim and his family had left New Zealand and settled in Australia in 1980. With encouragement from Jim, my parents applied to emigrate to Australia and were approved in 1982. I gathered that this was a country almost as far away from home as New Zealand. I assumed they would take me with them and I had mixed feelings about going to a strange country. Besides how could I cope with a very long journey on an aeroplane when I was not happy about travelling even within this country in a car? I had no idea where Australia was or how far away it was, but I realised that I could not go there by car.

Ron had told the official at the Australian High Commission that although his parents were quite happy to sell up and emigrate, he would prefer to see what the country was like before he did so. Ron was given a six months working holiday visa to visit Australia.

When Ron left for Australia, Mum recruited a young woman called Nicole to work as her assistant in both the advertising and the recruitment agencies. A few days after she started Mum and Dad went off to Venice for five days leaving her in charge. She was a bright young woman who survived this baptism of fire and served the businesses well over the next few years. I showed Nicole that I liked her by sitting on her desk and making it difficult for her to do her job.

Ron went off to stay with Mum's cousin in California for six weeks in December 1982 en route to Australia. He stayed with Mum's brother Jim and his family in Melbourne before moving to Sydney. After an extended stay, Ron returned in September 1983 but Dad learned that there was no longer a demand for his skills in Australia so they could not emigrate. Needless to say, I was very pleased at this news and breathed a huge sigh of relief. My relief was tinged with sadness for my parents who were looking forward to migrating to Australia.

While he was in prep school Ron began to show an interest in playing the drums. His parents bought him a few drums to start with but by the time he boarded in Sussex, they had bought him a decent set of drums which he took with him to the school. In fact they had to buy a larger vehicle in order to carry Ron's drums which would not fit into their present car together with his trunk. Ron's favourite genre was "Heavy Metal" and his parents accompanied him to live concerts performed by Supertramp, Status Quo and Led Zeppelin.

After leaving boarding school, Ron formed a band which used to play in pubs in and around Reigate. As he had ambitions of becoming a professional drummer, he had the drums shipped to Australia so he could take them to auditions. Listening to other contenders at an audition in Melbourne, Ron realised that the others performed much better than he and decided not to pursue drumming as his career. His drums had to be shipped back to England when he returned. He continued to play the drums for relaxation for several years in our barn at "Benting Mead" (our next house move).

After Ron passed his driving test some time in 1981, his parents bought him an American car. One day I was sunning myself in the front garden when I was rudely awakened by the loud roar of the powerful engine of a Chevrolet

Camaro. While Ron was in Australia, Mum and Dad got rid of this car and bought a brand new Ford Fiesta which they gifted to him when he returned.

Ron's girlfriend Louise came from Australia to live with us early in 1984 and the two of them toured Europe in the Ford Fiesta that summer. Ron was very disappointed with its lack of power so he changed it for a sporty Triumph Stag.

A few months later, Ron and Louise brought home a female Siamese cat whom they named Ella. I was very put out by her arrival. For one thing Ron transferred all his attention and affections to Ella and for another I could not bear to listen to her constant plaintive mewing which got one my nerves. I lost my privileged position as sole pet overnight and I had to resign myself to my new situation of an also ran.

Ella

One day Ella went missing and the whole household was frantic with worry. They were searching for her everywhere in the vicinity. Our garden backed onto the playing fields of the local Sixth Form College. A couple of evenings later Mum accompanied by Ron and Louise continued their search in the school premises. When they called out her name Ella answered with a plaintive "meaow". After about an hour they found her cowering in the bushes near the main school building. She was very frightened and did not venture far for several weeks.

When Ella was older I took her under my wing and we became very good friends. She was grateful to have an older cat teaching her the ropes. We became so
friendly that Ella used to sleep cuddled up next to me.

Mum and Dad tended to dabble in property. They bought a shop premises in Nutley Lane, Reigate that had a studio flat at the back. They obtained change of use to an office which they rented out. The studio flat was refurbished and sold.

Following a re-organisation within the organisation that Dad worked for, he received a promotion to Business Systems Manager and

Deputy Head of the Management Services Division. In December 1984 Mum and Dad decided to visit Australia and Sri Lanka on a five weeks holiday. I was quite alarmed that I would be sent to the cattery again with no Tammy to keep me company. My fears were soon allayed because Ron and Louise stayed in the house and Ron looked after Mum's businesses which now had several employees.

My parents spent some time in Melbourne followed by about a week touring and sharing the driving with Jim. They visited Canberra and the Blue Mountains, and Bondi beach in Sydney. They also visited Louise's mother Lizzie in New South Wales and returned to Melbourne for Christmas and to see in the New Year with Jim and his family. They spent a couple of nights at the Raffles Hotel in Singapore on their way to Sri Lanka where they had a grand party for their friends and relations in January to celebrate their twenty fifth wedding anniversary.

Mum and Dad decided to move to a larger house in Reigate and so put up our house for sale. When prospective buyers came to view the property, Ella used to go along the wall ahead of them, clinging to the hessian wall covering. This was a source of amusement to

Hercules and Ella

the viewers but unfortunately it was also a distraction. I never attempted to climb on to the hessian as I was too heavy.

The purchase of our new home in Reigate was completed in July 1985 although the present house had not been sold. Louise's mother Lizzie came over from Australia for the summer. The two of them accompanied by Ron as the driver, went off on a month long motoring tour of Europe. His parents bought Ron a used Ford Cortina and had it overhauled for the trip. On their return, Lizzie helped Mum and Dad to clean up our new home in readiness for our move.

When we moved to Benting Mead, Ron and Louise stayed on in Chart Way so that the house would be lived in and also to show prospective purchasers round the house. As Ron still had his Triumph Stag sports car, my parents let Louise have the use of the Cortina.

Chapter 4 - Benting Mead

In October 1985 we moved to "Benting Mead", also in Reigate, about three miles away from Chart Way, near a village called Woodhatch. Dad and Ron moved the furniture themselves in several trips in a hired van. Ron and Louise continued to live in the house in Chart Way with Ella to show prospective purchasers round.

The purchase price of the new house was more than double the sale price of the Chart Way house, so financing the purchase had been difficult as a large loan was required. Ultimately an insurance broker was able to arrange a loan. As the house in Chart Way had not been sold, Mum and Dad had to obtain a bridging loan from their bank.

Not only did our new home have a spacious front lawn but a huge back garden with lots of trees and shrubs with fields all around. This was my idea of heaven. I could sun myself on the lawn, climb trees, try to catch birds and roam anywhere I liked to my heart's content. The previous house was sold three months later and Ron, Louise and Ella moved in with us. Like me, Ella too was delighted to see many trees in a large garden.

A few months after we moved into Benting Mead, Ella was mated with a pedigree Siamese and in March 1986 she gave birth to three male and three female kittens. One female, a Chocolate Point died in a day or two before she was named, and when they were old enough, Ron found homes for the other two girls, Georgie a Chocolate Point and Simmi who like Ella was a Seal Point. The three tom cats were a Seal Point Sammy, a Blue Point Barney and a Lilac Point Tristan.

After Tammy's disappearance I reigned as the sole pet of the household for over three years. This had been ended by Ella's arrival and I was quite upset by it. Ron and Louise's attentions were totally focussed on Ella and I had less attention from Ron. Mum and Dad continued to favour me over Ella.

I had just about got used to having Ella around and had become very friendly with her before she gave birth to this large litter. I soon realised that I had to share the family's, even my parents' attention and affection with the three kittens who remained. However I used to get my share of petting and cuddling whenever I wanted to.

When I wanted a cuddle I used to wander into the sitting room where Mum and Dad were watching television, and jump on to Mum's lap. Mum used to still love to cuddle me, but I kept myself to myself most of the time. If I wanted my tummy tickled I used to lie on my back in Mum or Dad's presence and they would oblige. In the summer I used to sit for long periods on the front lawn just under the hedge.

Tristan and Barney on cooker hood

I still loved climbing trees and trying to catch birds who played their part in teasing me and flying within my reach. I was now twelve years old and not as quick as I used to be so the birds were able to evade me more easily. It really was a young agile cat's game and I had grown too old to enjoy it.
I had nothing to do with the kittens although I was still quite friendly with Ella. I could not

help noticing the antics that the kittens got up to as they were growing up. There was a gap between the wall cupboards and the ceiling of the kitchen and some of them used to get up there and sit with one paw hanging over the edge. Visitors used to be startled to see movement at that level and even more surprised when a kitten used to suddenly jump down from that height and land safely on the worktop. I was too old and too heavy to indulge in such activities.

Another change occurred in the spring of 1986 when Mum and Dad decided to get a dog. This was partly due to security as Benting Mead was quite isolated. Mum had been keen on a German Shepherd dog but Dad had reservations. His attitude had been influenced by the fact that when he was a child he had known of several households where a German Shepherd dog had attacked members of the family. It had taken

Dad several years to realise that the dog must have been provoked in some way. We now had such a large garden in which a dog could exercise as an alternative to being taken for a walk. The dog they chose was a Rough Collie whom they named Bertie although his Kennel Club name was "Titus Tiberius Tarquin".

Dad was a fan of P G Wodehouse, so Bertie was named after the Wodehouse character Bertie Wooster. Bertie was very laid back and would not hurry for anything. He also hated walking into water or on any shiny surface such as floor tiles. Bertie befriended the kitten Barney and would pick him up in his mouth and carry him about like a mother cat would. I do not think Barney liked this very much but had to put up with it as he was so little.

Dad made a small square wooden bottomless box for each of the Siamese cats. Each of these was placed on an electrically heated pad before the bedding was put in. The cats revelled in the warmth from these heated pads. They never climbed into my parents' bed. I had been well used to finding my own warmth wherever I could, sometimes even on Mum and Dad's bed, so I was not too bothered that I did not get a box. I had more fur than the Siamese. Anyway I would have had to have a larger box for which the heated pad would have been too small.

Ron and Louise had gone off to Australia to spend Christmas with Lizzie when my parents brought home another puppy. Dad had withdrawn his objections and the new puppy was a German Shepherd who was named Kipper. The name Kipper was also based on a Wodehouse character named Reginald Herring whose nickname was "Kipper". At eight weeks old Kipper was a bundle of fur with large paws when he arrived in December 1986. Perhaps his large paws were an indication that he would grow to be a very large dog. Kipper was very different from Bertie, full of energy and always rushing around. We had snow that winter and the two dogs had a great time frolicking in the snow. I did not like the snow, I much preferred to be curled up in a warm place.

Ron was attending university in Central London and finding the travelling quite time consuming. He was also frustrated that he could not spend time in London with his fellow students socially. He and Louise were looking for a place to live in London. They bought a flat in Putney in March 1987, but they left the kittens at Benting Mead as their lease prohibited the keeping of pets.

While I was sunning myself on the front lawn one summer's afternoon, a strange man appeared. He attacked the front door which broke open, and entered the house. He came out a few minutes later carrying a bag. Bertie followed him out of the house as he had left the front door ajar. Mum had taken Kipper to her office to get him used to car travel. Perhaps if Kipper had been there the burglar may have thought twice about entering the house. Although not yet fully grown, Kipper was a large and intimidating German Shepherd dog.

One day Sammy was found with serious injuries to his face, with part of the skin hanging loose. Mum and Dad thought he had been attacked by an animal, but when they rushed Sammy to the vet, they were told that his injuries were consistent with being hit by a vehicle. The vet did a wonderful job sewing the skin back on Sammy's face and he made a full recovery from this very traumatic incident.

I have stated earlier that Bertie used to carry Barney about in his mouth. As he got older, Barney was not frightened of the dogs. He got his revenge on Bertie when he was much older by sitting on a bar stool in the kitchen and taking a swipe at Bertie as he passed by.

On several occasions, I saw Barney do this, sometimes even taking a swipe at Kipper.

Tristan was nervous around the dogs but was emboldened by Barney's actions. He thought this was fun and jumped on to an adjoining stool and imitated his brother in harassing the dogs. I did notice that the two kittens indulged in this daring activity only when a human was present in the kitchen. Perhaps they were clever enough to know that they would be rescued if the dogs decided to retaliate.

I noticed that all the Siamese cats always seemed to go back in the house to use the litter tray although they had a large garden in which to relieve themselves. I never came indoors to do my business even when it was raining. I can't remember whether Tammy taught me to do this, perhaps she did.

Both Sammy and Barney developed a respiratory problem which baffled our vet who referred them to the Veterinary Hospital in Bristol where they spent six weeks undergoing tests. I can't imagine how poor Sammy and Barney felt on their very long journey of over a hundred miles each way, with stops of course. Their condition which was incurable but manageable, was attributed to the fact that their parents were closely related. At the time that Ella was mated Ron did not know this.

Mum had to have major surgery in August 1987 and as she would have to be away from work for about three months, Dad resigned from his job in April to help run the businesses. In September while Mum was still recuperating, they went off to Sri Lanka to celebrate Grandpa and Grandma's fiftieth wedding anniversary. Soon after their return, Mum decided she needed more time off work and thought it would be a good idea to go back to Sri Lanka and spend some time with her parents.

Mum was to leave on a Sunday in October, and the previous Thursday night there was an almighty storm which lasted all night and disturbed my sleep more than once. When Mum and Dad woke the following morning they found that both the electricity supply and the telephone service had been cut off as a result of the storm. Luckily we had an open inglenook fireplace so this was lit to provide heat. Dad retrieved a double burner gas stove and gas canisters from the barn for boiling water for washing and for making tea.

As stated before, the office was now in a maisonette which, therefore, had a bath/shower and cooking facilities. The office was very near Reigate town where the electricity and telephone services had been unaffected by the storm so Mum and Dad went there to shower and watch television. They had takeaway meals for the three days before Mum left for Sri Lanka.

Dad had a tough time for a couple of weeks following the storm. He had to live alone in a house with no electricity or telephone and look after two dogs and five cats. He had to light his way inside the house with a torchlight. In the mornings he would feed us animals and breakfast on cereals and tea before leaving for work. He used to return at lunchtime to let the dogs out for exercise. In the evenings he used to feed all the animals before going out to shower, dine and watch television in the office. Dad used to return home late to sleep in a cold house.

A very alarming incident occurred the day the electricity supply was restored to Benting Mead. The morning after the storm, Dad had turned on one of the plates of the ceramic hob but had failed to turn it off. He had subsequently placed the gas stove on some newspapers on top of the hob with the gas canisters by its side. When the electricity supply was reconnected, the live plate of the hob set fire to the newspapers on which Dad had placed the gas stove. It was a great stroke of luck that Dad happened to be in the kitchen when this happened so he was able to turn off the hob and knock the flaming newspapers to the floor where they scorched the Flotex floor covering.

I dread to think of the consequences if Dad had not happened to be there - the house would probably have burnt to the ground with the dogs in it. Us cats would have escaped through the cat flap.

As both businesses continued to expand Mum and Dad decided to purchase the freehold of an office building in Nutfield with enough parking space for a dozen cars. The building was refurbished and altered internally to suit the needs of the businesses. There was an opening ceremony followed by a celebratory party attended by the press and several clients, most of whom came from London, when they moved into the office in May 1988.

When I heard that my parents were off again to Australia that summer, I was terrified at the prospect of us cats, five in all, being put in a cattery because Ron and Louise were no longer living in Benting Mead. The two dogs too would have to be put in kennels. I was so relieved when Margaret, a friend of Mum and

Dad's who lived in Scotland, came down to look after the house and animals. Ella and her three sons had never been in a cattery so they did not know any better, but what a relief it was for me. Margaret was very kind and seemed to love animals. I liked her and I think all the other animals did too.

A couple of days after Mum and Dad left on their holiday, Margaret had to call in an electrician because the plug points in the kitchen had stopped working. While the electrician was checking the connections, Barney jumped on the worktop and directed a jet of urine directly at one of the plug sockets, obviously as some sort of protest. The electrician was amused at this but now knew the cause of the short circuiting.

I was now old and feeling very tired. I was also slowing down in my movements and spent most of my time sleeping. I think I will hand over to Kipper to continue this narrative. At eighteen months old he has grown into a big dog and I am sure he will do justice to the continuing history of the family and their pets.

I had been a healthy cat who only visited the vet to be neutered and to have my annual booster vaccination. It was now 1990, I was sixteen years old and slowing down. I had lost some of my teeth and was finding it difficult to chew my food so Mum had to mash it up for me. Unusually I suddenly lost my appetite and my worried parents took me to the vet, a kindly bearded Scotsman. The vet kept me in overnight and I had a needle in my paw all night with some liquid flowing through it. Dad collected me the following morning. I still could not eat anything but was only able to drink water.

A day later the vet turned up at home and I noticed that Mum was crying as she cuddled me. I did not know what Dad meant when he said to Mum "Do you realise we may have to do this six more times". Dad took me upstairs to their bedroom followed by the vet and cradled me in his arms. The vet lifted up the skin in my neck and I felt a prick.

KIPPER

Chapter 5- New kid on the block

Let me introduce myself. I am Kipper a long haired male German Shepherd. My Mum and Dad call me "Kippy". Hercules has already described how I came to be called Kipper. I was born in October 1986 and my sire was "Vassendorf the General" who, I heard had been imported from Germany. According to Kennel Club records my sire belonged to Richard Starkey (better known as the Beatles' drummer Ringo Starr) and his wife Barbara Bach. This connection is my claim to fame.

I had some brothers and sisters but particularly remember one brother. When Mum and Dad first came to where we were with our mother, my brother ran up to Dad and I ran up to Mum. Of course I had no idea at the time why these two people had come to see us but we were both picked up and cuddled. A day later Mum and Dad came again and took me to my new home in Benting Mead.

Bertie

I am taking up this narrative from Hercules, the large black and white cat who had been with the family since 1973 and sadly passed away in

1990. Hercules kept himself very much to himself not fraternising with the other cats except Ella. I think he felt a bit left out after the birth of Ella's kittens. Although Hercules gave us dogs a wide berth I was sad to see him go.

I was eight weeks old when I arrived at Benting Mead. There was already a dog there named Bertie, a rough collie who was about six months old and therefore bigger than I, although it was not long before I outgrew him. There were several cats - a big black and white called Hercules, a Siamese called Ella and Ella's three sons, Sammy, Barney and Tristan. All the cats kept their distance from us dogs except Barney who fearlessly moved close to us. He never ran away if either of us approached them in a friendly manner but stood his ground. Tristan sometimes plucked up the courage to imitate Barney in harassing us dogs from the safety of a bar stool. The three brothers were characters each in their own right as Hercules has described earlier.

As Bertie was older he took me under his wing but as I grew older and larger I became the boss. Bertie was very laid back and also had a fear of water and smooth surfaces. After rain there used to be several puddles of water in the garden. I used to happily run into puddles and play in the water but was never able to coax Bertie to join in. It snowed heavily about four months after I came to Benting Mead. Bertie and I had a fantastic time playing in the snow. Although he kept well away from water, snow did not seem to bother Bertie at all and he joined me enthusiastically.

While we were both still puppies, Bertie would attack and rip any upholstered furniture while I fancied getting my teeth into anything plastic including the television remote control. Mum and Dad had to replace two remote controls which had been savaged by me. When there were no humans in the house to watch us, the doors to the sitting room and office/library were kept shut. A bar stool was placed across the foot of the stairs to prevent us from going upstairs. The stool stayed in place for several months until my parents were satisfied that Bertie and I understood that we should not be going upstairs.

The full moon held a strange fascination for me. While I was still young I went in the garden one night and on seeing a full moon I started howling at it. Perhaps this was caused by the wolverine genes of my ancestors - the wolves who are famed for baying at a full moon. My parents were quite alarmed and started calling me into the house. I realised that my endeavours were not having any effect on the moon but I continued to do the same whenever I saw a full moon.

I was terrified of very loud noises, especially fireworks. One or two nights a year during winter, there was prolonged noise from fireworks for several hours. I used to be so frightened that I used to break the rules and run upstairs to safety and cower under Mum and

Dad's bed. I heard the family referring to one of those events as Guy Fawkes night.

The first holiday that my parents took after I came to Benting Mead was to Sri Lanka after Mum's major surgery. Ron and Louise were looking after the house and animals and during this time I "got out of nappies". In other words I stopped doing my business on the newspaper provided in the house and started going outside the house for the purpose.

As we grew older and stronger Bertie and I began breaking through the chicken wire fence which surrounded the inner garden. Bertie used to look for weaknesses in the fence and with my superior strength I used to force a way through. Several times we escaped on to the road and Dad had to come looking for us and coax us to come home. Dad had to spend a lot of time continually repairing the fence. As I grew bigger I used to jump over the fence which was about four feet in height so Dad had to attach angled brackets to the posts and fix chicken wire to them to stop me from doing so.

As I was a bad traveller, Mum used to take me to her office for a morning or an afternoon to get me used to car travel. One afternoon, we came home to find the front door of the house open and Bertie in the front garden. I heard Mum tell a friend that some items were stolen from their bedroom. The front door had been forced open. I think I worked out what may have happened. I had no doubt that Bertie would have barked his head off but as we had no near neighbours, no-one would have heard him. The bar stool would have prevented Bertie from following the intruder upstairs. I wondered if I would have been able to intimidate the intruder had I been at home. One will never know.

After they moved to their flat in Putney, Ron and Louise were unable to look after us, so Margaret, a friend of Mum and Dad used to come down from Scotland to do so. Once she brought her elderly mother down for a fortnight. Margaret used to sometimes have friends over for the weekend. She had come to stay with us before and I liked her. I once greeted her in the front hall on her arrival by standing on my hind legs and placing my paws on her shoulders. Unfortunately, I knocked her over. I suppose that was not surprising as I was now by all accounts a big dog and did not know my own strength. I was careful not to do this to anyone again. Margaret helped Mum and Dad out over several years by looking after the house and animals when they were on holiday.

I was a proud dog and undisputed leader of the animals in our home. One day I was near the barn when I saw a large Rotweiller in our field and my hackles rose so I ran under the strands of the barbed wire fence to confront him. As I approached ready to chase him off our land, Major turned to face me and glowered at me. It was a battle of wills and I soon conceded that

Major was "top dog". We quickly became friends and whenever I managed to escape from our garden we went hunting together in Benting Woods which was behind our property. I once caught a chicken, and not knowing what to do with it, took it home as a present for my parents. Dad gave the chicken to a neighbour, Major's owner, who presumably killed and ate it.

The garden was large so there was plenty of room for us dogs to run about for exercise. Sometimes we amused ourselves at the expense of walkers on the public footpath that separated the garden from two large fields which formed part of the seventeen acre property. We used to run along the length of the fence barking at them until they were lost from view.

Sometimes my parents would throw balls in the garden for Bertie and me to retrieve. I used to chase after and retrieve the first ball thrown but would not let go of it when asked to do so. The ball had to be prised from my mouth. Mum or

Dad used to show me another ball and say "Bertie's ball" before throwing it. While Bertie started ambling after it I used to rush past him and retrieve the ball. I was so selfish that Bertie got to retrieve a ball only if I was restrained by my collar while he ran after it.

Bertie and Kipper

Mum was a keen gardener but due to lack of time she had to engage a knowledgeable gardener who came once a week. If Mum was working in the garden I would not sit by her but at a discreet distance from where I could survey most of the garden. If Mum was in the green house I would move close to it and sit outside.

As both Mum and Dad were very busy with their jobs and in maintaining the garden, we dogs did not get many walks with them except at weekends or on summer evenings. Bertie and I did not meet other dogs except at our weekly dog training classes, so I was always excited when I came across another dog on our walks and used to strain on my lead to go and fraternise with it.

Dad was not strong enough to hold me back and had to resort to tethering me to a lamp post or telegraph post when other dogs were passing us. Another thing which used to excite me and cause me to take off was the sight of a squirrel. Bertie showed no excitement at all when meeting other dogs and showed no interest in squirrels either. I must say that when Mum took Bertie and me out on her own we were much better behaved and did not try to drag her. I used to drink water from a stream while on our walks but my parents soon realised that my stomach was getting upset whenever I did this so they stopped taking us there.

One day when Mum and Dad were out grocery shopping, I wandered into the kitchen to find the door of the refrigerator wide open. Barney was hovering around so perhaps he had had something to do with the refrigerator door being open as it was very unlikely that Mum or Dad had not shut it. I got the smell of meat and quickly located some steaks which I managed to retrieve and eat. I was so greedy and selfish that I did not give any thought to sharing it with Bertie. I also found and ate a packet of butter.

When my parents returned, they worked out from the wrappings on the kitchen floor that something had been eaten by one of the dogs, the obvious suspect being me. Quite by chance, that evening while Mum and Dad were in the kitchen, Barney walked up to the refrigerator. He stood up on his hind legs and used his front paws to open it, exposing himself as the culprit of the earlier incident.

The following day Dad bought a child proof lock for the refrigerator. The staff at Mothercare had been very amused when told that the lock was to prevent a cat and not a child from opening the refrigerator. Anyway, the following evening the family was in the kitchen waiting to see what Barney would do. Barney tried opening the appliance in the same way as before, standing on his hind legs. When he failed, he lay on his back under the refrigerator door and used all four paws to try to open the refrigerator, again unsuccessfully, so he gave up. What a clever cat!

Barney had also worked out that the bonnet of a recently arrived vehicle was warm, so he used to sometimes be found stretched out on the bonnet of a car until the engine cooled. I was really amazed at how clever Barney was.

Tristan too had his quirks. Mum had often observed him sitting on the roof of our large outbuilding which we referred to as "the barn". On some occasions he would suddenly stand up on his hind legs and appear to claw at something in the air. Mum was puzzled by this but one day she realised that Tristan acted like this only when an aeroplane was flying overhead. As we lived quite close to Gatwick airport there were plenty of aeroplanes flying in the area. Mum worked out that Tristan was trying to catch a big "bird" just as he would attempt to catch birds in the garden. The whole family found this quite amusing.

The three Siamese tom cats had another ritual. If they heard my parents' car returning they would rush from wherever they were and clamber up the stairs. When Mum and Dad opened the front door, they usually found the cats sitting on the stairs, each on a different step like a tableau to greet them. Mum used to call out to the cats by name, sometimes from an upstairs window. Even if they were out in the fields they would come dashing across the fields to wherever she was.

On one of our annual visits to the vet for my booster vaccination, my parents were told that at sixty four kilograms (one hundred and forty pounds) I was far too heavy. The vet suggested that my weight should be reduced for health reasons. This meant that I was given less to eat and was always hungry. I was a big dog and needed my food but I suppose reducing my weight was good for my health. When I was weighed a year later my weight had come down to fifty five kilograms (one hundred and twenty one pounds). My parents thought this was a great achievement but at what cost to me?

Bertie and I were never given tinned dog food. We used to get dry food in the morning but for our main meal in the evening, whoever was looking after us, used to painstakingly cut raw carrots and celery and feed it to us with green tripe and cooked rice. Sometimes we used to get left overs from the family's meals as well. I loved eating carrots although I found that they passed through my system undigested. Whenever Mum or Dad took some carrots out to feed the horses, I used to follow and keep harassing them till I got my share.

One evening a workman Steve, having finished his work for the day, was having a cup of tea in the kitchen with Louise before going home. Steve was amused to see Dad cutting up vegetables which he thought was for the family dinner. Noticing Steve's interest, Louise said "that is not for us, it is for the dogs". Steve replied "Blimey it looks better than what I will get for my tea when I get home".

There used to be a milkman driving down

Lonesome Lane in his float every morning whom Bertie and I disliked. We used to hear the milk float at quite a distance and kept barking until it passed our house and faded into the distance. There was also a little Yorkshire Terrier who used to go along the road with his owner past our house for a walk. Their destination used to be the public footpath that ran through our property. As he passed, he made it a point to enter our front garden and do his business in a flower bed. This bed was just over the gate between the front garden and the back garden where Bertie and I were. We could not stand this affront but despite our ferocious barking the little dog took no notice and defiantly continued to trespass whenever he was passing.

One day Dad noticed that the little dog's owner was letting him run free in one of our fields instead of keeping him on a lead on the public footpath. Dad went out to confront the person who was trespassing. I remember Dad checking the gates before he went out to make sure that Bertie and I were confined to the garden.

I was convinced that there was going to be trouble when Dad confronted the trespasser. I broke through the chicken wire fence, charged towards Dad at top speed and was at his side even before he got to the trespasser. Dad was very surprised to see me there and appeared to be worried that I might attack the little dog who had been acting cheekily in our front garden. Dad need not have worried because although I looked fierce, I was really a softie. Dad warned the man that he was trespassing and we returned home.

Because our garden was so large Mum and Dad had bought a ride-on lawn mower. The grassed area consisting of the front and back gardens, excluding the orchard took about four and a half hours to mow. Sometimes a gardener used to do the mowing but at others Mum or Dad did it. Mum was a keen gardener and she had several flower beds and an enclosed vegetable garden in part of the orchard. She once won a prize at a local village show for the largest marrow. On the recommendation of a landscape designer Mum planted about forty specimen trees.

Mum's brother Winston who was a good mechanic was visiting Benting Mead and Dad took him into the barn to look at the ride on lawn mower which had been giving trouble lately. I followed them into the barn. When Dad started up the machine inside the barn it made very much more noise than it did when it was outdoors. The problem was that it kept stopping after a few minutes. I somehow got it into my head that this loud machine was going to harm Dad. I kept barking to warn Dad but he ignored me and kept starting the machine every time it stopped. After a time I got so desperate that I nipped Dad in the abdomen sufficiently to hurt him and at last he took notice. I used to sometimes use this ploy to attract Dad's attention if all else failed.

Although I was menacing in appearance and Bertie was docile and laid back, Bertie is the one who actually showed aggression on occasion. Ron used to often have his friends visiting and they used to move back and forth between the barn or the outer garden and our enclosed garden. While we were having our meal one evening, one of Ron's friends was coming to the house from the barn. Instead of entering the garden through the gate, this young man decided to climb over it.

In a flash Bertie left his meal, dashed over to the young man and bit him in the buttocks. Bertie probably thought that a friend would have opened the gate instead of climbing over and so considered this person an intruder. Bertie's intervention took all of us by surprise and luckily the young man only suffered from shock as the bite had not broken his skin. I never bit anyone in anger. I only nipped Dad when I wanted to draw his attention and this is the method I used whenever I wanted Dad to let me out of the house into the garden. I never did this to anyone else.

Bertie and I were taken to dog training classes in Guildford during my first summer at Benting Mead. I was growing fast and the trainer who used to train Police dogs once said "Kipper I will buy you a saddle when you grow up". During the winter we were taken to an indoor training class in Reigate. Bertie was terrified of tiled floors for fear of slipping and he also avoided stepping into any water, preferring to walk round a puddle while I would rush straight in.

During the indoor classes I used to sometimes escape from the building and roam about outside in the dark. I don't know why I did this but it meant that Dad spent a lot of time looking for me and calling my name until I decided to give myself up. Frankly, I was a rather disobedient and wilful dog. I obeyed only when I wanted to.

Life at Benting Mead was my idea of heaven. The large garden enabled us dogs to run around for exercise, chase birds and squirrels and bark at people using the public footpath which ran through our land. The cats did their own thing, mostly remaining indoors but occasionally wandering outside to enjoy the sun on warm days. During my second summer, Dad decided to take Bertie and me for a walk before he left for work. As we walked out of the gate on to the lane, Dad found two of the cats, Barney and Tristan, following us, so fearing for their safety, Dad decided to walk us round our eight acre field for the rest of that summer. Barney and Tristan continued to follow us but they were safe.

Mum was scheduled to undergo a serious operation in August 1987 and anticipated being away from work for a few months. Dad resigned his job in April and joined Mum's businesses. Dad's fiftieth birthday was in October but as Mum was away in Sri Lanka recovering from her surgery, the celebrations were postponed till the following month. The party was held in the barn and was well attended with several relations and friends coming down from London for the "bash" on a Saturday evening.

Hercules has already mentioned the great storm of October 1987 following which there was no electricity for ten days. Mum went off to Sri Lanka to continue her convalescence following her surgery so Dad was left to look after the businesses, the house and us animals. It was late October and it got dark quite early. Dad used to return from the office, feed the animals and go back to the office which was in a maisonette with bath/shower and cooking facilities as the electricity supply there was in place.

He used to dine, shower and watch television there before returning home to a cold house quite late.

When Dad came home to feed us one evening accompanied by a friend, he found that Bertie and I had shut ourselves in the through lounge. We were normally shut out of this room when nobody was at home. That lunchtime Dad had not shut the door properly, so we managed to get into this large room. Somehow or another we got ourselves shut in. We became frantic because we could not get out. I kept scratching at the door trying to open it and gouged the wood quite badly. When Dad returned he had great difficulty in pushing the door open as in my panic I had ripped the carpet off the floor and it was blocking the door. When he finally managed to get into the room he found the carpet ripped through the whole thirteen foot width of the room. This was a good example of how strong I was. Fortunately Dad was able to use the large pieces of carpet elsewhere.

Dan, the stepson of Dad's brother Guy and now aged nearly twenty one, came to stay with us. He had left home and gone to Australia for a few months. He had his belated twenty first birthday party in the barn at Benting Mead where Dad had had his fiftieth the previous year. He got employment in a local catering company and stayed with us for over two years until he married Vicky and moved out.

Dan was quite fond of Bertie and me and would even take us for walks sometimes. He was much stronger than Dad and was able to restrain me when I decided to take off after a squirrel or fraternise with other dogs during our walks. Dan did not like the cats very much so he never stroked them or picked them up.

Ron graduated from University in 1988 with a Bachelor's degree in Film and Videographic Art. He had set his heart on a career in the film and television industry. Ron had got a taste for it while making animated films with Grandpa when he was about eight years old. He started work almost at the bottom of the ladder as a freelance Clapper/Loader.

I used to rush around all the time, running everywhere at top speed. As I said before, Bertie was very laid back and would not run unnecessarily while I was like the so called "bull in a china shop". The shattered glass from a broken window in the barn had been lying near the gate between the stables and the adjoining paddock. I used to often run to this gate to bark at the horses or their owners who were wandering about and had trod on some of the splinters of glass which were lying around. I felt no pain, but Mum examined my paws and found several pieces of glass embedded in them. She decided to take me to the vet to have them removed. All the pieces of glass were removed under anaesthetic, the first time I was given one. I heard Mum telling Dad that I had alarmed both her and the vet by taking some time to come out of the anaesthetic.

The year 1989 was the family's "annus horribilis". Early in the year Ron was diagnosed with cancer and underwent surgery. Fortunately, he did not have to follow this up with any chemotherapy or radiotherapy treatment. Later in the year, Mum's biggest client whom she had signed up after the office moved to South Nutfield, went into liquidation, forcing her advertising agency to follow suit. As the recruitment agency was still doing well, Mum was able to finance the setting up and operation of a new advertising agency.

Grandpa (then aged eighty one) had been admitted to hospital in Sri Lanka suffering from breathing problems. Mum made a flying visit to see him, spending only thirty six hours in the country and returning to attend a creditors' meeting. Grandpa made a full recovery.

In the mid 1990's Margaret was not able to come down from Scotland to look after the animals as her elderly mother and aunt needed constant care. During this time my parents used to go on holiday separately to Sri Lanka to visit Mum's parents. On one of these occasions, when Dad was away, I fell seriously ill and had to undergo major surgery. I learned later that I had been neutered and had had my spleen removed together with a quarter of my liver. I never underwent surgery again.

Grandpa and Grandma came for short stays in the early 1990's on their way to and from Florida to visit their younger daughter who had emigrated there. Bertie and I were always happy to see them as they were dog lovers. They had some Pomeranian dogs of their own in Sri Lanka whom they both, particularly Grandpa, doted on.

Chapter 6 - Difficult Times

Hercules was the first pet in the household to pass away. On a cold winter day in February 1990 Dad dug a hole in the frozen earth of our front lawn to bury him. I saw Dad struggling to dig but he managed to dig deep enough for a grave. He planted a Cherry Blossom tree in the grave with Hercules and filled it up. The following evening Dad blacked out with a severe pain in his upper left arm and was taken to hospital in an ambulance. The doctors suspected a heart attack as Dad was fifty two years old and somewhat overweight. He spent a few days under observation in hospital where they carried out some blood tests and monitored his heart function. The results showed no sign of a heart problem so the doctors decided that the pain was caused by a muscular problem.

I was very protective of my Mum and Dad as you would expect a pet dog to be. I have related the story of my going into the field to protect Dad when he confronted a trespasser. If

Mum was in the house alone, I used to follow her from room to room and lie down watching her. If she kept moving frequently I used to show my impatience by sighing loudly. If a man, possibly a salesman or tradesman, came into the house in Dad's absence, I used to announce my presence with a growl and then stay very close to Mum while they were there even if I had seen them before.

Around May 1991, Sammy one of the Siamese cats who suffered from respiratory problems, appeared to be struggling to breathe. He had to be rushed to the vet quite often but he did not appear to get any better. Mum probably feared the worst so she started spoiling him with treats. Sammy's favourite food was prawns. My parents put a plastic thing on his face with a tube leading from a metal cylinder. I heard that they were giving Sammy something called oxygen which was stored in the metal cylinder to help his breathing. Margaret was visiting and she tearfully implored Mum to have Sammy

Sammy

put to sleep because she saw that he was suffering. I heard Mum talking about placing Sammy in an "oxygen tent".

Despite the oxygen, Sammy's breathing became more laboured and he had to spend a couple of nights at the veterinary surgery. When he returned home and smelled the home smells, he seemed very excited and, although weak, he virtually jumped out of his pet carrier as soon as it was opened.

Sammy passed away later that day and I heard Mum say that the longest day of the year had been poor Sammy's shortest day. He was buried in the garden and as in the case of Hercules, a tree was planted on his grave. Mum had gone out with Ron so Dad and Louise were there when Sammy breathed his last. The whole family mourned Sammy's passing.

Sammy and his brother Barney had been quite close but after he died, Barney became very attached to the surviving brother Tristan. They used to sleep cuddled together and used to go everywhere together. In short, they were inseparable.

Tristan and Barney

George, the older son of Dad's brother Jay who had been studying in New York, came to stay with us for six months in early 1992. He loved to drive Dad to the office in the old Ford Cortina and helped out in the office during his stay. His parents had been approved to migrate to Canada so he joined them and his brother in that country the end of his stay with us.

Ella passed away in 1993. Mum had noticed that Ella was unwell when she found her lying very limp on the flagstone in front of the open fireplace. It was evening and Ella was rushed to the vet where she was kept overnight. In the morning Mum was told that despite the best efforts of the veterinary staff, Ella had died. They suspected that Ella had been bitten by an adder. I heard Mum saying that there had been adders in our garden because one of them had been found dead some years ago, having got entangled in some chicken wire.

I had heard my parents discussing the purchase of the office premises in South Nutfield in 1988. Their plan had been to rent out the premises after the mortgage was paid off, so that the rental income from the premises would provide them with a comfortable pension. Alas, this was not to be due to circumstances beyond their control. Both businesses, particularly the recruitment agency, suffered a severe downturn in revenue in 1992/3. My parents were forced to let all but one of their staff redundant and surrender the office premises to their lender. Mum decided to run her businesses from the barn at Benting Mead.

The businesses had been able to weather previous downturns because they had been operating on a smaller scale and Dad had been in full time employment. My parents' only sources of income had suddenly dried up and, for the first time in his working life, Dad had to claim unemployment benefit.

The advice offered by lawyer and accountant friends was to sell Benting Mead and pay their debts. There was enough equity in the property to provide a sufficient surplus for a house deposit. My parents felt that being in their midfifties with hardly any income, they would not be able to borrow to buy another property even with a substantial deposit. They decided that their only asset, Benting Mead, had to be saved at any cost so they set about finding other sources of income.

Mum consulted their friend Tony, the builder who had worked on their house in Chart Way, who had just returned after living in Spain for five years with his wife. Tony suggested that the fields should be turned into paddocks and the stable of four loose boxes should be re-furbished with part of the barn being turned into a tack room. This enabled my parents to earn some income from "do it yourself" liveries. Tony converted the side of the barn closest to the house into an office, kitchenette and toilet for use by the office staff. Mum began running her two businesses from this office thus saving on rent/mortgage repayments and business rates. My parents were very grateful to Tony for his practical suggestions and his offer to defer payment for his labour. Tony remained a much loved and valued friend.

Mum decided to sell the advertising agency to the only employee who remained and to concentrate on the recruitment agency. She had to build this business up all over again changing the types of occupation she was dealing with. Income from the business was uncertain and together with the rent from the liveries hardly enough to live on. My parents were unable make the monthly mortgage payment on Benting Mead and fell into arrears.

We animals were all very happy that both Mum and Dad were around most of the time as Mum was now working from her office in the barn. Dad was at home and spent his time writing job applications and helping Mum with the accounting and administration sides of the business.

Bertie and I hardly ever ventured into the office. If we did, we were soon ordered out. While Mum was in the office and the house was empty we "stood guard" in the garden. A favourite pastime of ours was barking at walkers on the public footpath which ran along the eight acre field. Whenever Mum returned to the house I used to follow her in. The office was about sixty yards behind the house so we always barked to warn of any approaching vehicles or people turning up at the front door of the house.

As Hercules described earlier in his narrative, the Blue Point Siamese cat Barney was quite a character. He now started doing something new. If he found Mum setting off from the house in the direction of the office or the main barn, he use to leap off the ground to perch on her shoulder like a bird. Even when Mum was at her desk in the office, Barney used to drape himself round Mum's shoulder. I thought his antics were quite amazing.

One day a lady accountant was visiting her client who now owned the advertising agency. Bold and inquisitive Barney went on to the desk she was sitting at and sat in front of her. The silly woman who probably knew nothing about cats, blew into his face in a friendly way.

Barney surprised everyone by leaping at the woman's face in retaliation and scratching her. Luckily the scratches were superficial and the woman was not badly hurt.

After the incident where Bertie and I shut ourselves in the through lounge, Dad used to sometimes leave the door wedged open when they were out. One day they came home to hear music blaring out of the music centre. When I heard the music I wandered into the room to find Barney sitting on the music centre and the other cats seated close by, all listening to music. It transpired that Barney had accidentally trod on the buttons of the music centre while wandering about on the shelf. Once Barney worked out what made the music start, he would once in a while walk on the buttons even when my parents were at home. That is how Mum and Dad discovered what had been going on. Barney really was an exceptionally clever cat.

As the liveries were earning them hardly any money, my parents turned their attention to the house. They got Tony to convert the small back bedroom upstairs into a kitchen and installed a door half way up the stairs to make the first floor of the house into a self-contained flat which they were able to rent out. There was already a toilet downstairs and the old boiler room was converted to a wet room with a shower. My parents moved downstairs, using the former study/library as their bedroom. The upstairs, now with its own kitchen was let out.

I was very concerned when I saw strangers moving in upstairs and even more when others came to visit them. This made our job of guarding the house and our parents even more difficult but Bertie and I were up to the task and nothing untoward happened during the time the upstairs was tenanted.

Dad, now in his mid fifties had been unemployed for over a year and had great difficulty finding even casual work. He saw an advertisement for a part time book-keeper aged over forty five years for a local company. He was lucky to get that job in the late summer of 1993 and spent five and a half happy years with that company.

Good Friday in 1995 was a very bright, sunny and warm day at Benting Mead. I heard Mum calling Tristan as he was not in the house. Tristan normally came when mum called. When he did not respond, Mum came into the garden and headed towards the barn where Tristan sometimes hid. As was my wont I followed Mum towards the barn and we found Tristan lying in the sun and struggling to breathe.

Mum realised that Tristan had not long to live so she picked him up and cradled him in her arms. She sat there for over an hour until he breathed his last and I sat with her the whole time. It was frightening to see Tristan struggling for every breath and I dreaded to think of my suffering in the same way when my time came. As with Hercules, Sammy and Ella, my parents buried Tristan in the garden and planted a tree on his grave.

I hated going to the vet. I was always happy to jump in the car for a short journey but I did not know we were going to the vet until we were nearly there. Bertie had his annual "booster" vaccine at a different time to me so I was all on my own. Once we got into the veterinary surgery I used to cower under a chair and tremble much to Mum or Dad's distress. Uncharacteristically, I ignored all the other animals that were brought in although the dogs sometimes barked at me and made aggressive moves. I was very scared when I was at the vet's but I never struggled when handled by the vet or pricked with a needle. Except for my visits to remove splinters of glass from my paws and major surgery to remove my spleen, I only went to the vet for my booster vaccination.

Barney

As Ron had separated from Louise he decided to sell their flat in Putney in 1996. He posed a problem for
his parents by asking if he could stay at Benting Mead until he bought another place. They still depended on the rent from the upstairs of the house as part of their income so there was no room for Ron. However, Mum came up with

the idea of converting the double garage into a studio flat for Ron.

Tony was called in to build a toilet/shower room, and install kitchen worktops, sink etc . with the requisite plumbing and the necessary electrical connections for white goods. Ron lived in this "annexe" for ten months before he bought a house in North London. The annexe was then rented out.

Barney, the blue point Siamese cat was put to sleep on Mum's birthday in 1997. Barney had a long standing respiratory problem caused by in-breeding but survived for over eleven years. He was pre-deceased by both Sammy and Tristan although the latter had only shown symptoms of the problem long after his brothers. Barney too was buried in the garden and a tree was planted on his grave.

Mum really missed having a cat, especially one as clever as Barney. About three months later

Mum brought home a three year old Siamese female seal point cat called Nancy from a rescue centre. She was now the only cat in the house. She was very affectionate towards Mum and kept well away from Bertie and me. Nancy was a timid cat but soon settled in and appeared to feel very secure in her new home.

My parents had tenants upstairs for four years until the income from Dad's part time job and from Mum's business increased sufficiently to be able to meet all their commitments. In the meantime they were able to gradually increase their monthly mortgage repayments on Benting Mead.

Margaret began visiting us again after her mother passed away. She now had a little Border Collie dog called Geordie whom she had rescued. After some barking time spent conveying the message to Geordie that this was our home and that he was only a visitor, Bertie and I tolerated him. We both liked Margaret but her petting us or giving us our food did not go down well with Geordie. This young upstart actually flew at Bertie and me and attacked us viciously. We were taken by surprise and had to defend ourselves.

The dogfight was stopped by Tony who happened to be doing some building work in the house. Nobody else in the house could have stopped this fight which would have certainly ended in bloodshed. I think Margaret got Geordie's message and was very careful not to pay too much attention to Bertie and me during the rest of their stay.

By now Mum's business was improving and with more money coming in she and Dad decided to build a further four loose boxes for "DIY" livery. Having obtained planning permission, the job was entrusted to Tony who was assisted by Graham. They came from Hastings and stayed over three nights a week going home mid-week on a Wednesday night.

My parents were to go to Sri Lanka in December for the early January wedding of Winston's daughter Diana and Ron was to look after the house, animals and business. During a visit to Winston's house with Jim, Diana invited Ron to her wedding and he decided to accept. Mum and Dad had to hastily arrange for house/animal sitters and left the business in charge of an employee.

The house sitters were an elderly couple. They decided to take Bertie and me for a walk one day, the man taking charge of me and the woman of Bertie. The man soon found that he was not strong enough to control me and the walk had to be abandoned. Anyway Bertie and I got plenty of exercise running about in the large garden. The couple realised their limitations and did not attempt to walk us dogs again.

I heard that Diana's wedding in Sri Lanka in January 1998 had been a spectacular affair, with the bride and bridegroom dressed in local costume and the latter arriving for the ceremony astride a caparisoned elephant. The spectacle had caused quite a stir among the guests at the hotel where the wedding took place with several of them recording the event on their cameras and video recorders.

It rained a lot that January and the garden was getting water-logged. I loved rushing around and splashing in the water but Bertie would not join in because he hated water. One day Bertie disappeared. Mum and Dad searched everywhere for him and even put up posters on trees and telegraph poles along our road. I learned that they had even been to a rescue centre in London thinking someone may have seen Bertie wandering about and taken him there. I thought this was unlikely
because Bertie's collar had a tag with the family's telephone number on it.
From the time that Bertie went missing I was quite lonely. Where had my friend and com-

panion of over eleven years gone? Why had he abandoned me? Had somebody snatched him?

Sky

All these questions went through my mind and I started sulking a lot as I missed my canine companion.

Late in the month Richard, a man who grazed his horses in our fields and collected the livery rents for my parents, reported that he had found Bertie dead in a ditch in one of our fields. Bertie hated water but had fallen into the ditch and could not get out because of mud. It was ironic that despite his hatred of water, Bertie met his end in a muddy, waterlogged ditch. Like all the deceased pets before him, an ornamental tree was planted on Bertie's grave in the garden.

A couple of months later, Mum and Dad took me on a longish car journey to a place which I later learned was a rescue centre, where there were a lot of other German Shepherd dogs. A lady came over one day from the rescue centre to vet my parents and check out the facilities and environment. On meeting me she commented that I was well looked after and remarked that the large garden was "dog heaven." A few days after this we returned to the rescue centre. This time we brought home a long haired German Shepherd bitch called Sky. I did not mind her lying in the car with me or coming to our house as I thought she was only visiting. We were both very quiet during the journey home.

Night came and Sky was still in the house so I got suspicious that she was here to stay. I was not amused and uncharacteristically started barking and lunging at her to let her know that she was not welcome. Mum and Dad put Sky in a separate room overnight but put us together again in the morning so I had to re-commence trying to get my message across again that she was not welcome. Was she trying to take Bertie's place? This time I actually attacked Sky who defended herself well. Yet, uncharacteristically I bit her and drew blood, prompting Mum to take her to the vet for treatment. I have said before that I am not vicious by nature - I don't know what got into me. Perhaps it was my grief at losing Bertie and not wanting any other dog to take his place.

Ultimately I had to accept that Sky was here to stay so I decided to make the best of the situation. I was over eleven years old and did not have the spirit to go on fighting. As time went on I managed to be friends with Sky who was several years younger than I and she even coaxed me out to the garden occasionally to play. I was visibly slowing down and did not have the energy to chase a ball at top speed as I used to. Besides, I missed Bertie terribly. He had been my "brother" and comrade in arms for eleven years.

It is said that dogs tend to be more attached to and protective of humans of the opposite sex. As I have said before, I was equally protective of both my Mum and Dad. Sky was different. She was very attached to Mum and was obsessively protective. She did not even like any of the other pets getting attention from Mum and used to growl jealously. Mum had to constantly reprimand Sky for this. Sky growled at every man she came across and even kept away from Dad. It took her about a year before she began to trust Dad. It was obvious that she had earlier been badly ill treated by a man. I sympathised with Sky's determination that she would not lose her new owner as she had lost her previous one.

What follows is a sad story I heard being related to some visitors. Mum's parents stopped over at Benting Mead on their way to Sri Lanka in June 1998. As they were unable to produce some documentation, the immigration officer at Orlando airport had told them to visit the US embassy in Colombo. The embassy cancelled their US visas as they had overstayed their six month visa by over a year.

Grandma was devastated that she could not return to her home in Orlando which she had furnished at what was to her a considerable cost. They had sold up all their assets including their house in Sri Lanka as they had thought that they were moving to the USA permanently. They had nowhere to stay in Sri Lanka so they came back to the UK and stayed with us at

Benting Mead for just over two years. Marie and her husband sponsored them legally and they returned to Orlando in late 2000.

Grandpa and Grandma occupied Ron's old room and Dad turned the front bedroom into a sitting room for them with a sofa and a television set. Grandma loved to watch sports on the television, particularly tennis and cricket, so Dad subscribed to a satellite network to allow her to do this. During their two year stay with us Grandma underwent surgery to replace her left knee.

Dad gave up his part time job in January 1999 to work for a company based in Reigate as full time Company Secretary and Accountant. I was happy to see Dad often coming home at lunchtime.

Throughout my life I used to get very excited if I saw Mum or Dad take my lead off the wall as

I loved going for walks. I found my walks with Mum, Dad and Sky more wearying as time went on. I could not walk very far at all. I used to have to turn back less than fifty yards into our walk. The spirit is willing etc. Sky was several years younger than I and had a lot of energy. As her walks were curtailed due to me, Sky used to get her exercise running about in the garden. At just under fourteen years, I was really getting very old and I tired easily. It was a struggle getting up in the morning from a lying position when Dad wanted to let me out. I spent most of my days lying down with no desire to stand up and walk about.

As my hind legs became weak and painful, I was having difficulty standing up from a prone position. According to our vet this weakness was common among German Shepherd dogs and in my case, was exacerbated by old age. He suggested to Mum and Dad that they should try acupuncture and recommended a vet in

Handcross who practised this discipline. Dad used to take me by car and had to help me to get in because my back legs were too weak.

The vet used to insert needles into various parts of my body and once or twice she even lit something to warm the needles up. I kept very still all the time mainly out of curiosity but also because the treatment did not hurt me at all. I felt better after the treatment and was very surprised that I was able to climb into the car without any help from Dad. It surprised Dad too as he had not been sure what to expect. Each time we went for this treatment Dad had to help me into the car but after the treatment I was able to get in by myself as my legs felt stronger.

One morning when Dad came to get me up I could not control my bowels and defaecated on my bedding. I could hardly stand but managed to struggle outside. Some time that afternoon Dad came home early from work. He carried me out into the garden outside the kitchen and sat down on the ground with me across his knees. I saw a man who had come the previously to treat one of the other pets. He was a vet. Dad asked the vet "how long has he got?" "Two days perhaps". Dad started crying and repeating "I am sorry Kippy, I am sorry Kippy". The vet bent over me. Suddenly the rest was oblivion.

NANCY

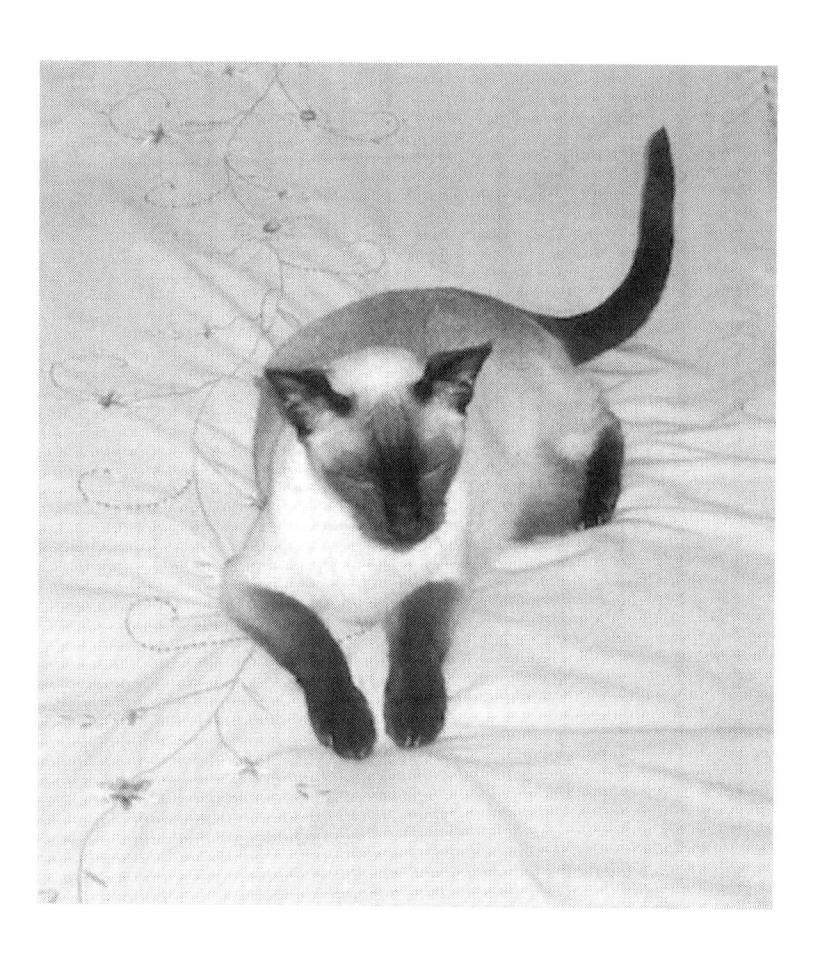

Chapter 7 - Rescued

I am Nancy and I am a three year old Siamese seal point female cat. I had been living happily with a family up to now but my owners' circumstances changed and they could not keep me any more. I was very sad because I loved the family. They took me to a place which had lots of other cats but they were all in enclosures. Each day one or two cats were taken away from this place by people and sometimes new cats joined us. I don't know how long I was in this place.

It was October 1997 when a kind lady who is now my Mum came and took me away by car on a long journey. I was taken to a house with a very large garden where there were already two dogs as family pets. I was the only cat and I learned later that the last of the family's five pet cats had passed away a few months earlier. Four of them had been pure bred Siamese cats.

I had had other cats for company in my previous home so I felt a bit lonely.

My previous home had a tall wooden fence on all three sides of the small back garden. Most of the garden was paved and there were no trees although there was a narrow strip with flowering plants. I could not see any large trees in the adjoining gardens either. Coming to Benting Mead was a revelation to see this large garden with trees, shrubs, flowering plants and fields all around. There was a wood nearby with large trees. I loved to see the leaves change colour on the trees when autumn came. I knew I was going to enjoy living in this place.

For eight of the fifteen years I spent with the family I was the only pet. Because of this the previous narratives by Hercules and Kipper will be hard acts to follow. It will not be full of anecdotes about what the pets, both cats and dogs got up to or the carefree time they had enjoyed in the vast grounds of Benting Mead. My account is more about the family's story rather than those of the pets.

There were no dogs in my previous home as my owners were essentially cat people. I was very wary of the two big dogs at Benting Mead although they appeared to show no interest in harassing me. I learned that there had been five cats already in the house when the dogs arrived so they had both got quite used to co-existing with cats.

The rough collie Bertie was found dead in a ditch a few months after I arrived. As the surviving dog Kipper appeared to be lonely and sulking a lot, Mum and Dad brought a rescued German Shepherd bitch called Sky to keep him company. After fighting her for a day, Kipper accepted that Sky was there to stay. I kept well away from these two big German Shepherds.

Sky was very close to and protective of Mum and used to follow her about as Kipper had done earlier. She would not leave Mum's side for a minute if Mum was on her own. She even growled at the other pets if they came near Mum and had to be often reprimanded for doing so. She probably wanted desperately to hold on to her new owner having lost the previous one. I noticed that Sky tended to keep away from Dad and greeted any other men who were around with a growl. She was very wary of Dad for almost a year after her arrival and obeyed his commands only reluctantly. I heard Mum say that she had probably been ill-treated by a man in her previous home. She ultimately accepted that Dad meant her no harm and allowed him to pet her.

I am afraid my former owner rather spoilt me with regard to my food. I was never given any cat food from a tin or packet (except for treats), only roasted chicken breast. Gourmet or what? This information had been passed on to the rescue centre who told Mum, so she continued to feed me roast chicken breast mixed with a few cooked vegetables which I found delicious. She sometimes used to give me cream or milk.

After a meal Mum used to sometimes give me a plate with a few left overs. I used to love to be allowed to eat the left overs and lick the plate even though they were other meat, fish or vegetable, not chicken. Roast chicken breast was always my main meal.

One day the chicken meal I was offered smelt different. I tasted it and the taste was different too, so I refused to eat it. I heard Mum tell somebody that she had given me meat from a chicken leg not the breast, and I had refused to eat it. What a spoilt brat I was!

A few months later Mum and Dad brought home a male Siamese blue point called Oliver who was about ten years old but very mobile. I heard Mum telling one of her friends about Oliver one day. He had been used for breeding and had later suffered from feline flu'. He had been kept on as a pet but his owner was trying to re-home Oliver. Mum had found him through a Siamese Cat Rescue Centre somewhere near Guildford. When they went to collect him he had gone walkabout and they had to hang around for some time before he returned. The minders were wondering whether he would return at all as he had only been brought there recently. Oliver was quite laid back and, perhaps because of his age, only moved fast if he had to.

I continued to be wary of the dogs and kept well away from them. Oliver, however, was fearless and daringly moved close to the dogs. I heard that one of the Siamese cats who had been earlier pets had been equally unafraid of the dogs. As I said before, the dogs left us cats alone but I for one was not willing to take any chances.

Oliver and I became great friends and used to clean each other's coats. We used to roam round the garden but never went outside the

Oliver

fenced area or on to the road in front of the house. We went hunting around the garden looking for field mice and even birds who would have flown into the windows of the conservatory and crashed to the ground.

The squirrels too used to interest us quite a bit as did the black birds who were always singing, mostly in the evenings, and flying about the arbour leading to the barn. In the Spring time there was always the scent of flowers from the various ornamental trees and fruit trees. Sometimes we used to sit in the orchard observing the birds but neither of us was interested in trying to catch them. I wonder whether it is abnormal for cats not to want to chase birds. Oliver was too old to leap at birds but although I was younger, I had no inclination to do so. In fact I never even jumped on to a table. I did sometimes get onto a chair in the conservatory to enjoy the sun.

Summer was a specially enjoyable time for Oliver and me. We used to spend hours in the shade of the trees in the orchard. The plum trees at the far end of the garden were laden with fruit and my parents used to invite people to pick them. The darker plums were usually attacked by birds but there were still enough left over for picking. The cherries on the tree in the orchard never survived the birds although Mum and Dad tried protecting the tree with a net. There was a surfeit of fallen apples from the several trees in the orchard some of which had also been attacked by birds. My parents were able to save and eat the pears.

Although neither Oliver nor I ever chased birds, Mum had tied bells to each of our collars so our movements could be heard by the birds. This made it quite difficult for us to play hide and seek as we could hear each other approaching from any direction. When I was upstairs in the bedroom and heard Oliver on his way upstairs from the tinkle of his bells, I used to hide behind a bedroom door and pounce on him as soon as he passed the door. Oliver in his turn, chased me up and down the long bedroom until he caught me and we began to play. We created a lot of amusement among the people in the sitting room downstairs when they heard us running across the wooden floor.

Kipper was quite old now and had some problem with his hind legs and Dad used to take him regularly by car for some treatment. Kipper appeared to be better whenever he came back from one of those trips. Sky tried her best to get Kipper out in the garden to play with her but poor Kipper was unable to participate fully. Eventually, Kipper had to be put to sleep at the ripe old age of thirteen years and ten months. I understood that this age was remarkable for a German Shepherd of his size.

My parents went to Sri Lanka in December 2000 for Ron's wedding to Alice and were away for two weeks. Margaret came down from Scotland with her dog Geordie to look after the house and the animals, namely Sky, Oliver and me. Margaret was careful not to pay too much attention to Sky and evoke Geordie's jealousy. I heard that Geordie had attacked Kipper and Bertie in the past through jealousy.

Mum and Dad went off again in February 2001 for a fortnight, this time to Australia to attend the wedding of Jim's youngest daughter. Ron and Alice who were on a round the world trip for their honeymoon, joined them in Australia for the wedding.

Margaret came again to look after us although it was only two months since she last came. What a good friend Margaret had been to my parents over the years in coming such a long way to look after the house and animals. Because of her, Sky, Oliver and I were spared the ordeal of going to kennels or cattery. Having spent some time in a refuge both Oliver and I, and Sky too, knew what it was liked to be cooped up in a cage.

Grandpa passed away in Florida in September 2003 aged ninety four. He had been in a care home suffering from dementia for about eight months. Mum , accompanied by Winston, flew to Orlando, Florida to visit their father in hospital a few days before he died and stayed on for his funeral. Mum sold her recruitment agency later that month and retired from working. After Grandpa's death, Grandma wanted to spend some time in England with my parents. Dad went to Orlando and brought her home to Benting Mead.

I lost my good friend and companion in February 2004 when Oliver who was nearly seventeen years old had to be put to sleep due to failing health. I really missed him as we had got on so well during the six years he was with us. I had been at Benting Mead only a few months before Oliver arrived and I had thoroughly enjoyed his companionship. Once he was gone I became the family's only pet cat.

I felt very lonely after Oliver passed away and there was no sign of my parents getting another cat to keep me company. Although I kept away from Sky I had the consolation of knowing that there was another pet animal around. In my loneliness I constantly sought human company. I used to love being in the same room as Mum or Dad and started jumping on to their bed at night to sleep with them. On particularly cold nights I used to sneak under the duvet for extra warmth.

Sky had to be put to sleep in August 2004 as her back legs had given way and she was unable even to stand up. I was now the sole pet in the household for the first time in twenty years. As there was no dog to be looked after, it was easy for Mum and Dad to put me in a cattery when they went away on holiday. Until now whenever my parents went away on holiday, someone had lived in the house to look after the animals. I had to resign myself to regular periods of being cooped up in a cattery. I was still able to enjoy wandering in the garden and listening to the birds on my own but it was so different from doing so in Oliver's company.

Although Mum and Dad had invited Grandma to stay with them for good, she said that England was too cold for her and wanted to retire to Sri Lanka. My parents took Grandma to Sri

Lanka to have her right knee replaced and to find her a suitable care home. A residential home run by Benedictine nuns offered Grandma a room so Mum and Dad extended their stay to furnish it and see her settled before they returned.

My parents spent Christmas 2004 and saw the New Year in with Ron and Alice in their home in the Wirral. They had woken up on Boxing Day morning to the devastating news that a tsunami had hit several Asian countries including Sri Lanka causing much destruction and the loss of thousands of lives. They had immediately telephoned to see if the Home that Grandma was in had been affected. Although the tsunami had damaged the coastal area of the town, Grandma's Home was further inland and had been unaffected. My parents had been very relieved to hear that Grandma was safe.

Mum and Ron had owned a freehold hairdressers premises in St. Leonards in East Sussex since 2000 with a maisonette upstairs. They sold the maisonette and bought a one bedroomed leasehold flat behind The Grand Hotel in Eastbourne for letting.

While Grandma was with us at Benting Mead, my parents used to take her for drives and day trips. When they returned from some of their trips, I used to hear them referring to a place called Eastbourne which they visited fairly regularly. It soon transpired that my parents had decided to retire to Eastbourne.

My parents decided to sell Benting Mead and buy a smaller property for their retirement. Major improvements and extensions were undertaken in order to make the property more attractive to prospective buyers. The former double garage, now a bedsit, was expanded by the addition of two bedrooms. A new double garage was built on the other side of the house from the original garage. A new building of four loose boxes was built by Tony facing the existing loose boxes.

As I loved the company of humans, I used to sit in the middle of the building site while Tony was putting up new buildings, carefully observing what he was doing. I kept at a discreet distance and out of harm's way. Tony was very fond of animals and used to often talk to me when he stopped for a cup of tea.

Grandma came over for a few months in 2005 and accompanied my parents on a holiday to Orlando (to collect some of her things), Las Vegas and Los Angeles where Grandma met up with some of her relatives. I heard that Grandma loved to play the slot machines in the casino of the MGM Grand Hotel in Las Vegas which she had visited several times with her daughter Marie during her stay in Florida.

There was a woman running a refuge for cats quite close to Benting Mead and she agreed to keep me while Grandma and my parents were away in America. Mum had as usual wrapped each meal in a separate packet for the duration of my stay. Mum had noticed the woman giving my specially prepared food to a nursing bitch. She thought this was a one-off incident and was shocked to find that I had lost a lot of weight when she came to collect me. I hated the food the woman gave me so I virtually starved for a fortnight. I was never taken there again.

At the age of eighty six grandma was quite apprehensive about travelling alone. Vicky asked one of her friends who was a stewardess on the flight to pay special attention to Grandma in Business Class and she returned to Sri Lanka for good in late 2005.

Over the next few years my parents went abroad on holiday several times and each time I was taken to a cattery. I had to accept that this would be a regular occurrence now that they had retired from work. They used to go to Sri Lanka once or sometimes twice a year to see Grandma in addition to their other holidays abroad. Mum used to prepare a sufficient quantity of my special food for the duration of their holiday and take it to be stored in the freezer at the cattery.

I missed being able to roam about in the garden but had to get used to these periods of confinement in a cage. Although there were other cats in the cattery, I could not fraternise or play with them as they were each in their own enclosure. My life without the company of another cat was now beginning to be a very lonely one. My only solace was that I was able to spend time with my parents whenever they were at home.

My parents had put Benting Mead up for sale. Late in 2006 a business couple with three children living in Reigate responded to an advertisement in the Sunday Times. They had viewed the property earlier before the latest additions and improvements. After a couple of further viewings they made an offer which Mum and Dad accepted.

The prospective purchasers were a couple who ran a business. They had two boys and a girl with ages ranging from eight to twelve. The house they were in had only a small garden so the children had a great time running about in the fields when they came for a viewing. They were very much looking forward to the acres of fields they could play in when they moved to Benting Mead.

There was a lot of preparation to be done for our move. Dad went through all the junk that was in the barn which had been collected over twenty two years. The junk included several items which had come from the loft at Chart Way (the family's previous home in Reigate) and the office in South Nutfield which had not been disposed of earlier. Dad made several trips to the local refuse tip in Redhill and even burnt several items in the garden. Dad engaged a man with a digger to bury the metal which remained after burning.

Prior to moving to Eastbourne when Mum was packing some personal items, I suddenly heard the sound of Oliver's bell and went running upstairs. Mum had kept Oliver's collar with the bell attached which I heard. For a moment I thought that Oliver was upstairs and ran upstairs. I was very disappointed to find that he wasn't.

A removals company was engaged to do the packing, transport and storage, so there was quite an upheaval while they were doing this. As Mum and Dad had not yet exchanged contracts on their new property in Eastbourne, most of the furniture and other possessions were to go into storage and we were to move into the little flat that they already owned in Eastbourne. A few days before we left, Mum went round the garden tying a tag with the name of each pet on the trees which were planted on their graves. We moved out of Benting Mead in June 2007.

Chapter 8 - Eastbourne (Harbour)

My parents and I moved to the little flat in Eastbourne two days before completion of the sale of Benting Mead. The Landlord gave them special permission to keep me in the flat for a short period. I thought the car journey was very long, much longer than when Mum brought me to Benting Mead from the rescue centre. Mum and Dad went back the following day as they had arranged for a professional cleaning of the house before the new owners moved in.

We spent seven weeks in the little flat before the purchase of our new home in Sovereign Harbour South was completed. Mum and Dad were out most of the day during this period leaving me all on my own. I suppose it was difficult for them to adjust to living in a tiny flat after spending twenty two years in a large house surrounded by so much land. I was looking forward to enjoying a garden once again when we moved to our new home.

I was very disappointed when our new home in Sovereign Harbour, Eastbourne, turned out to be a three year old penthouse flat on the sixth floor of a block of seventeen flats. Mum had placed a chair with a cushion on the balcony outside the master bedroom overlooking the sea. I used to sleep on this chair on sunny days and enjoy the warmth. Dad had taken the precaution of tying a netting to the railing of the balcony to make sure that I would not accidentally fall through it.

I missed being able to wander round a large garden but had got used to living in the confines of the little flat for seven weeks. This one was a large flat but despite my having several rooms between which I could roam, it did not compare with the ability to go into a garden. I had to accept that I would have to live my life without a garden.

Once in a way Mum used to put me on a lead and take me down in the lift to walk around the communal garden. I felt very uncomfortable in this communal garden which was surrounded by buildings and had a lot of parked cars around. I used to be frightened by the cars which drove by and some large dogs being walked in the garden. I would quickly indicate to Mum that I wanted to go home. It did not compare to being able to wander peacefully in the garden at Benting Mead surrounded by green fields.

Deprived of feline and even animal company, I had to seek that of humans to alleviate my loneliness. Although I never jumped up on to a table, I used to jump into my parents' bed while they were in it to enjoy their company. Whenever we had visitors I used to wander in to where they were and try to make friends with them. Most visitors were very kind, picking me up on to their laps and stroking me and telling me how beautiful I was.

When Mum and Dad were out, if I heard the key turning in the door lock, I would rush to the door and be there to greet them as they entered the flat. As time went on I was unable to hear so well except at close quarters and ultimately stopped going to the door at all. I was only able to greet Mum and Dad only when I saw them enter the flat.

Both my parents joined a local golf club and started attending ballroom dancing classes. They had to drive over five miles each way to the golf club, two or three times a week. The dance classes were more local but were still a car drive away. They went to the theatre regularly and those trips too involved a round trip of around seven miles by car.

The year we moved to Eastbourne, Mum and Dad went to California in August and to Sri Lanka in October to see Grandma and celebrate Dad's seventieth birthday. Dad was very happy to have had his two brothers and a classmate of his from 1946 at a celebratory lunch.

My parents holidayed in Europe quite often, mostly in the island of Tenerife where the temperatures were fairly constant all year round. I spent many months in catteries. As before, Mum always prepared sufficient food for me to be left in the freezer of the cattery. I had to get used to living for long spells within the confines of a cage.

We had visitors to stay over on a regular basis, mostly at the weekends. They loved the sea views from the sixth floor. Jim and Susan came over from Australia in the summer of 2008. After spending a week or so in Eastbourne, they went off with Mum and Dad to The United States and Canada for a fortnight. A few days after their return they set off again on a tour of parts of England which included a visit to see Ron and Alice in the Wirral. This meant that I was brought home from the cattery only for a few days before going back again. I was glad to be at home even for a few days.

Jim and Susan came again in 2009 when they joined Mum and Dad on a trip to Bruges and Brussels. They all went off to Sri Lanka to celebrate Grandma's ninetieth birthday in October with a grand party. Once again I had two spells in the cattery. By this time I had lost several of my teeth and found it extremely difficult to chew even the finely cut pieces of chicken breast. Mum saw that I was unable to eat much so she started pureeing my food. This made a big difference and I was able to eat my full meal again.

During our short stay in Eastbourne town, Mum and Dad had seen the advantages of living close to the shopping centre, theatres, pubs and restaurants. They had to travel by car to reach any of these places from where we lived in Sovereign Harbour so they decided to buy a place on the seafront in Eastbourne town.

Chapter 9 - Eastbourne (Seafront)

Our final move was to Eastbourne town in June 2010. Once again I had been hoping for a garden to roam about in and was bitterly disappointed. Our new home was a three bedroomed second floor flat overlooking the sea, near the Eastbourne pier. There were twenty one flats in the building.

My parents wanted to sell the harbour penthouse but as property prices had dipped following the financial crisis of 2008, they used it for holiday lets for the next three years.

Pets were not allowed in the new flat that we moved to, but because of my age the management turned a blind eye to my being there. Mum and Dad were told that when I passed away they could not have another pet in the flat. This flat was not as large as the penthouse in Sovereign Harbour but was equally close to and overlooked the sea.

The new flat needed a lot of work done to it. The two bathrooms and the kitchen were completely gutted and re-designed. All the kitchen appliances and white goods were replaced and the whole floor of the flat was boarded with the exception of the guest bedroom. The building work and plumbing were done by one man with occasional assistance. He took several months to complete the job and it was very unpleasant living in the dusty atmosphere.

Mum and Dad used to dress up in fine clothes regularly and disappear around nine o'clock at night for a couple of hours. I learned that they had gone to The Grand Hotel for some ballroom dancing. Some of my best quality time used to be spent with them on the settee while they watched television. On their return from The Grand Hotel, they always made a point of sitting with me to watch television so I was able to spend some quality time with them. The time I most enjoyed was sitting with them to watch television every evening.

I loved both my parents dearly and to show my affection I used cuddle up to Mum and lay my head on her lap for some time before switching to do the same with Dad. I used to swap between them as long as they were watching television. I heard Mum commenting to their friends about my routine, much to their surprise and amusement. She said I switched from one to the other every half an hour or so.

I had got used to sunning myself on a chair on the balcony in our previous home. This flat had an enclosed balcony with a wall about three feet high but fortunately it had a small window at floor level. Mum placed a cushion for me on the floor with a heated electric pad under it and I enjoyed the sun streaming through the window in the mornings.

After the building work and re-wiring of our new flat was completed, the whole flat was re-decorated. All the walls and the doors were painted white. This made what was previously quite a gloomy flat very bright. I was so relieved when the work was completed as I am sure Mum and Dad would also have been, after living in a chaotic and dusty environment for about four months.

We had several visitors to stay, particularly at weekends. Mum and Dad regularly entertained small groups of their neighbours in the same block of flats. Just before Christmas they used to invite all the residents and some friends from outside as well for a party. I enjoyed moving among the visitors and being picked up and petted by them. Most of them appeared to be animal lovers.

Dad had been complaining of abdominal pains for some weeks before his doctor sent him for an X-ray which was followed by a CT scan and a colonoscopy. Although he did not find any growths, the consultant was not happy with an unexplained inflammation in the colon. Dad underwent surgery at the end of May 2012 and was in hospital for about ten days. Not only was I missing Dad during that time, but had to spend most of the afternoon and evening alone while Mum went to see him in hospital.

The surgeon found a large tumour on the outside of Dad's colon which had been missed during the CT scan. I heard Dad say that he owed his life to that consultant because analysis of the tumour showed that it was malignant. Dad started a six month course of chemotherapy in July and both he and Mum gave up playing golf although they continued with their ballroom dancing. My narrative will end half way through Dad's treatment.

I was by now quite deaf and could only hear sounds very close to me. At nearly eighteen years old, my sight was also failing and I was weak and skinny. I was finding it difficult to walk. My parents' took me to the vet about once a month for a few months and she pumped some fluid into me to keep me going. During this period I spent a lot of time with my parents. When they were not at home I spent almost all my time asleep.

One Sunday, as I was feeling very unwell, I was seated on Mum's lap as she telephoned a vet to come and treat me at home but no one was available. My parents took me to the vet soon after. I thought I was going to have the fluid pumped in again but noticed that the vet was handling different equipment. As I was standing on the table I just about heard the vet asking Mum to support my head before she injected me.

Epilogue

Except for Tammy who disappeared, all our pets were buried in the garden of Benting Mead and an ornamental tree was planted on each grave. We were not able to do this for Nancy as we were living in a flat with not even a communal garden. As Nancy was getting old, my wife approached the General Manager of our golf club and asked whether we could bury Nancy in a rough area of the golf course.

He agreed to our request and we donated three native English trees which were planted to form a triangle. When Nancy died in September 2012, we buried her in the middle of the triangle. Whenever we play golf we stop by and say hello to her.

My wife and I continue to live in retirement on the Eastbourne seafront. We are grateful for having enjoyed the privilege of having pet dogs and cats for nearly forty five years and learning their various foibles. We look back with a mixture of joy and sadness for the wonderful time that we spent with them.